Praise for See You on the Internet

"One of the most comprehensive marketing guides to making your business known online that I have read. Highly recommended."

Bruce Croxon, tech investor at Round13 Capital & former Dragon on CBC TV's *Dragons' Den*

"I've read a lot of business books, but this one takes the cake. *See You on the Internet* is 200 pages of pure gold filled with actionable steps I can implement in my business—today. An absolute must-read."

Rachel Kelly, founder of Make Lemonade

"Understanding how digital marketing and media works is now more critical than ever before. In this book, Avery Swartz cuts through the acronyms and technical jargon, takes you by the hand, and guides you through the key concepts in an easy and accessible manner."

Allan Dib, global bestselling author of *The 1-Page Marketing Plan*

"I loved that reading the book felt like sitting down with Avery Swartz in person and being guided through the process. This book and its resources are exactly what entrepreneurs need to know about digital marketing, all in one accessible and practical place."

Paulina Cameron, CEO of Forum for Women Entrepreneurs

"A fun and accessible approach to digital marketing. Whether you're a complete beginner or years into running your own business, *See You on the Internet* uncovers the foundations of digital marketing that will grow with you and your business even as technology evolves."

Melissa Sariffodeen, co-founder & CEO of Canada Learning Code

"Your one-stop digital marketing shop! Easy to digest and practical AF. I wish a guide like this existed when I started my business."

Sarah Vermunt, founder of Careergasm & bestselling author of *Careergasm* and *Career Rookie*

"This is the book I wish every one of my clients (business owners) would read. It's full of easy-to-digest, practical information that situates the reader not just in what to do with their digital marketing, but also in how to think strategically about what they are doing. The conversational tone, real-world advice, and simple exercises make *See You on the Internet* an invaluable tool for every entrepreneur."

Danielle Botterell, principal of Spark Consulting

"I have run global marketing for some of the biggest and brightest start-ups. The complex landscape of digital marketing can make it hard to know where to start. *See You on the Internet* is a practical guide that walks you through a custom plan that's right for your business."

Melissa Nightingale, all-around badass

see you on the internet

avery swartz

see you on the internet 👋

building your small business with digital marketing

•• **PAGE TWO** BOOKS

Cataloguing in publication information is available from Library and Archives Canada.

ISBN 978-1-989603-08-6 (paperback)
ISBN 978-1-989603-09-3 (ebook)

Page Two
www.pagetwo.com

Cover design by Taysia Louie
Interior design by Fiona Lee
Printed and bound in Canada by Friesens
Distributed in Canada by Raincoast Books
Distributed in the US and internationally by
Publishers Group West, a division of Ingram

20 21 22 23 24   5 4 3 2 1

seeyouontheinternet.com

Contents

Introduction 1

Tech is supposed to make things easier, right? *3*
Measurement isn't meaning *4*
The missing link *5*

1   **A Framework for Digital Marketing** 7

A simple plan *8*
What the framework looks like, in practice *12*
Spin the wheel again *13*
What happens if you skip the process? *15*
From 30,000 feet to the weeds... and back *17*

2   **Domain Names, Email, and Hosting** 19

What's in a domain name? *20*
How the sausage gets made *22*
Registering domain names *23*
Hosting your website *27*
Email on all the things *28*
Chapter 2 from 30,000 feet *31*

3   **Yes, You Need a Website** 33

Planning and measuring website success *35*
Hiring someone to make your website *37*
Creating your own website *44*
Selling stuff online *49*
Chapter 3 from 30,000 feet *55*

4   The Three Components of a Modern Website: Mobile, Fast, and Accessible 57

Modern websites: Mobile and responsive *59*
Need for speed *63*
Accessibility: The web for all *63*
What do you like on other websites? Do that. *66*
Chapter 4 from 30,000 feet *67*

5   Lock It Down: Digital Privacy, Data Security, and the Law 69

A PICNIC (problem in chair, not in computer) problem *71*
How to protect yourself *72*
Your customers, your responsibilities *77*
Chapter 5 from 30,000 feet *84*

6   Content Is King 87

Throw away the elevator pitch *89*
Don't forget about the robots *91*
You do you *93*
Images *93*
Words *94*
A blog is not the only form of content *98*
Make it work *100*
Chapter 6 from 30,000 feet *101*

7   SEO 103

The billion-dollar secret: How does Google work? *105*
Black hats aren't going to help *107*
The three components of SEO *108*
How I did it: The Camp Tech story *113*
Chapter 7 from 30,000 feet *116*

8   Social Media 117

Which social media platform is right for you? *119*
Choose wisely *125*
What to post on social media *125*
15 ideas for social media content *126*
Social media culture and etiquette *130*

If you don't have something nice to say... *132*
Social media management tools *133*
Social media measurement *135*
Chapter 8 from 30,000 feet *136*

9 **Email Marketing 139**

Strategy, once again *141*
Who wants to hear from you? More people than you'd think *145*
What goes in the email? *148*
Think like an email recipient *149*
Email services that can help *151*
Okay, let's get started *152*
Test, test, test *154*
Campaigning for the outcome you want *156*
Chapter 9 from 30,000 feet *158*

10 **Online Advertising 159**

Advertising decision-making *162*
Platforms and costs *164*
Now that you've thought long and hard *168*
Start low and slow *168*
Chapter 10 from 30,000 feet *169*

11 **Keeping Track and Measuring 171**

Keeping track of customers and clients *171*
Metrics, metrics everywhere *175*
Chapter 11 from 30,000 feet *185*

12 **Bringing It All Together 187**

We're all the same *187*
Your digital transformation *189*
It's go time *192*

Acknowledgements 193

Index 197

Introduction

I HAD NEVER FELT so stupid in my life.

A few years ago, I had to transition to new accounting software for my company, Camp Tech. Like many small business owners, I tasked myself with the day-to-day bookkeeping for the organization and hired an accountant to do the big jobs, like preparing our corporate tax return. The software I had been using for bookkeeping was woefully inadequate, and a migration to a better system was long overdue.

At first, I tried workarounds and hacks. I looked for third-party software that would somehow take the mess of five years of fuzzy bookkeeping and magically morph it into the new accounting system. Unsurprisingly, I couldn't find any. I asked our administrative assistant if she could "just take care of it." That didn't work, because I couldn't give her the guidance she needed.

I realized I had to do the core work of moving Camp Tech's books to a new system myself. Once I understood it, I could teach someone else, but not until I had a firm grasp on the process.

It. Was. Painful.

Of course, I saw the irony of the situation. I own a company that teaches non-technical people about technology. Helping learners get through the tough spots and past the stumbling blocks of software is what we do. In this situation, I wasn't the teacher. I was the learner. And I have to admit: I hated it. It drove me bonkers, sitting for hours on end, struggling with software.

It wasn't really the software that I had a hard time with—I'm pretty tech savvy. It was the core concepts underneath. I had never learned accounting basics and never been given a framework for thinking about accounting. I knew that money came in and out of our bank account, and it needed to be accounted for, but beyond that I was pretty clueless.

Thank goodness the bookkeeper at my accountant's office was so kind and patient with me. She could sense my frustration and did her best to help. We spent many hours sitting side by side as she walked me through the details of double-entry accounting, and many more hours exchanging emails when I would forget half of what she taught me.

Eventually, I got it. And I even kind of like bookkeeping now. I finally understand it, but I had to go through the pain to get here. I had to listen, learn, and relearn, and I had to call my own deeply held assumptions into question.

In learning about the digital world, you may feel the same way. I have empathy for this process, and I know how challenging it may feel. You may be feeling insecure, unsure, and stupid, and there may be a giant voice in head saying *you can't do this.* But, like me, *you can do this.*

Tech is supposed to make things easier, right?

I've heard it said that there's never been an easier time to start a small business, because of all the technology at our fingertips. It's true! The barriers to setting up a business are lower now than they were 20 years ago. The internet has made it faster and cheaper to start a business, find clients or customers, and sell products or services to them. Technology puts the "mighty" in a small but mighty business.

While technology can be enabling and empowering, it can also be wildly confusing and frustrating. There's a moment that happens at every single Camp Tech workshop, regardless of the specific subject we're teaching that day, when it feels like a support group. One person expresses the frustration they felt trying to learn a tech skill on their own, and the sentiment ripples around the room. It is a classroom after all, and people are there to have access to a tech expert who will confidently and assuredly walk them through the particulars of a digital concept. People usually show up at Camp Tech because they've tried to learn something on their own, and it didn't go so well. I love that moment when everyone realizes, hey, we're in this together. And together, we're gonna get through it.

It's for these moments that I started Camp Tech in the first place. In early 2012, I picked up on a trend. I was working as a web designer in my own boutique web studio, and many of my clients were asking me a similar question. I would help them get their website up and running, but they wanted to know about all the other parts of bringing their business online. What about social media? SEO? Google Analytics? Email marketing? Most of my clients were small businesses and non-profits, and they couldn't afford to outsource all this stuff to a digital marketing agency. They wanted to learn how to do it themselves and asked me if I could refer them somewhere. In Toronto in 2012, there was nowhere to send them. No company was offering practical and accessible digital skills training. I'm talking about "learn it on Tuesday, use it on Wednesday" style classes. Not a semester-long course with lots of technical theory. Just the important stuff someone needs to know to get a job done. I saw a need and an opportunity and acted on it. Camp Tech was born.

Now, many years later, Camp Tech is still offering practical and accessible digital skills training in our Toronto classroom. We're also training people in other locations, through our group training initiatives, in communities across North America.

Measurement isn't meaning

One of the contradictions of our modern digital world is that we have access to so much data, but we have so little understanding about what it means. We're *drowning* in data. It seems everything—from the number of clicks our website receives to the number of steps we take in a day—can be measured. But measurement doesn't equal meaning.

For businesses, the sheer amount of data available from digital marketing efforts is baffling. We have so much information at our fingertips. It's overwhelming and often misleading. You can periodically glance at website analytics and social media metrics and see numbers that seem good. But are you sure?

People ask me all the time, "Is this a good number?" My response: I don't know! I don't have enough information to answer that question. I'm not sure what your situation is, so I don't even know if it's the metric you *should* be looking at, let alone if the number you have is a good value.

The missing link

The reason why it's so hard to find meaning in digital metrics and measurement is because you're often lacking two things: confidence and context. There are so many numbers to look at that we lack the confidence to know if we're even looking at the right metric and value for our situation. That leads to doubt and insecurity, which is not a great way to feel about digital marketing—something that's supposed to help us business owners, not confuse us.

And when you do look closely at metrics and values, you're often looking at numbers out of context. This is a big mistake! Digital marketing metrics have to be tied back to the most important thing—your business goals. If you don't know where you're hoping to go, how can a metric tell you whether you're getting there? If you can't see the correlation between digital measurement and your business goals, then you're lost. The numbers have no meaning.

Luckily, I know what you need. You need a framework for planning, executing, and measuring digital marketing. In this book, I'll walk you through the framework I use for my own small business and the one we recommend to others at Camp Tech. This is the missing link that so many business owners crave. The best part? The framework isn't complicated. It makes a heck of a lot of sense, and anyone can apply it to their business, no matter what the size, because it scales.

I'll use some examples to illustrate the framework and how it can be applied, and I'll also share some anecdotes from my own small business. If you're like me and you're old enough to remember the Hair Club for Men commercials from the '80s, where the man in the commercial said, "I'm not only the Hair Club president, I'm also a client," then you'll understand this analogy. I'm not just a small business digital advisor... I'm also a small business owner myself. I'm right here with you, friends. Let's get started.

A Framework for Digital Marketing

THERE'S ONE THING I see all the time with the organizations I work with. It doesn't matter what type or size of business—I see this clear across the board, from the one-person home-based businesses all the way up to companies with hundreds of employees across multiple locations.

Many people are missing a framework for thinking about and evaluating their digital marketing efforts. Without a framework, digital marketing can seem confusing at best—and like a big expense and a time suck at worst.

The messages out there about tech for small business are all about ease. "It's never been easier to start a small business—tech makes it so simple nowadays, anyone can do it!" or "You don't need to know about websites, our unique artificial intelligence algorithm will build it for you!"

I'm all for automation and making things easier... but not at the expense of understanding core concepts. And when it comes to a core concept of digital marketing—how to properly measure your efforts, so you know what's working and what's not—well, you can't automate that away.

A simple plan

The framework I use for getting started in digital marketing is deceptively simple. It's a series of steps, and it looks like this:

1 Set your goal
2 Choose your KPI
3 Measure (before)
4 Leap
5 Measure (after)
6 Learn

Let's briefly explore each step.

1. Set your goal

You have to start with your business goal. What do you want to achieve, at a high level? "Make more money" is an obvious goal that most businesses have. Be a bit more specific, though. Something like "make more money by selling a new product to our past customers" is a great business goal. So is "make more money by increasing the number of client projects we take on this year." The best goals are specific, measurable, and actionable. If you can clearly state what you're trying to do, in detail, then it can likely be achieved with the help of digital marketing.

2. Choose your KPI

Once you have your goal, make a plan for how you'll measure it. DO NOT SKIP THIS STEP. It is so important to set your plan for measurement *now*, not after you've tried some digital marketing activities. That's because it's easier to identify what you'll be looking for before you've started. After you've started, you can get distracted and it's too tempting to change your mind.

When it comes to digital marketing, there are all kinds of metrics and values you can use to measure your success. It can be totally overwhelming and paralyzing. That's why it's essential to focus on just one metric—the one that tells you whether you're getting any closer to your goal. That one metric is your *key performance indicator (KPI)*.

Try to pick something quantifiable for your key performance indicator. If your business goal is to increase sales, that's a great KPI. You will focus on the number of sales you receive, which is definitely measurable. Other quantifiable metrics that make for strong key performance indicators include: percentage of new clients versus returning (if your goal is to drum up new business); number of website visitors (if your goal is to drive traffic to your site); and number of clicks on a Google Ad (if your goal is to attract new customers who may be searching for a business like yours).

Remember that not all metrics are digital. Your key performance indicator could be something in the offline world, like the number of visitors to your store.

Everyone's KPI will be different, because everyone has different goals. The important thing is to pick one that corresponds with *your* goal. There are examples throughout this book to help you understand.

3. Measure (before)

Take a measurement of where you currently stand, using your KPI as your yardstick. How many sales do you presently have? What's the current percentage of new clients versus returning? How many website visitors do you have now? How many clicks are you receiving on your Google Ads (if any at all)? What are the engagement numbers (e.g., of comments, shares, likes, or follows) on your social media channels?

The purpose of this measurement isn't to inflate or deflate your current position—it's to be honest. Don't be embarrassed. And don't lie! You can't know how far you'll go if you don't put your stake in the sand and declare a starting point. This doesn't need to be complex. You've already identified your key performance indicator that will tell you if you get closer to your business goal. Take that KPI, check it against your current position, and write down the result. Be sure to save it—you'll refer back to it later to see how far you've come.

4. Leap

The next step is to leap. Why "leap" and not "plan"? Because when you are first getting started with digital marketing or trying a new digital marketing channel, there are a lot of unknowns. Yes, you should try to figure out as much as you can before you get started (that's what this book is for!), but there will be a certain amount of throwing spaghetti at the wall to see what sticks. You won't yet have any experience to draw from, so you just have to jump in and start your marketing campaign. But it's not a total shot in the dark—you're making a calculated first step.

I recommend not making a *giant* leap. Don't spend a lot of money or time at this stage; you're trying something out to see if it works. Start small and get the results. If your measurement shows some success, great! Double down. If your measurement shows you didn't hit a home run right out of the gate (much more likely), then you can adjust your strategy in the next cycle.

5. Measure (after)

Measure properly. What do I mean by "properly"? I mean you should look at the KPI you laid out for yourself when you set your goal. This is the step that requires the most discipline and honesty. You will be tempted to look at other metrics. You might even feel confusion and doubt that you picked the right metric as your KPI in the first place. Don't get distracted by the other things you could be tracking. You set your key performance indicator already, so only look at that. The emphasis here is on the word "key." Looking at other metrics is a distraction at best, and a lie at worst. Don't start looking at another metric because the value is higher, or it makes you feel better because it *seems* more successful than your KPI. The only purpose of looking at metrics is to learn, so you can improve. It's not to make yourself feel good.

6. Learn

After completing these steps, you've probably learned a lot. Take your KPI measurement and compare it to the measurement you had before you started your digital marketing campaign. How did you do? Are you any closer to your business goal? If you were to do the steps again (spoiler alert: you will), what would you do differently? What would you do the same?

What the framework looks like, in practice

I like to take the parts of the framework and lay them out in a chart, so I can clearly see them all. This doesn't need to be complicated! You could replicate this chart in a spreadsheet program or in a notebook.

Here's what it looked like for a health food store I worked with.

Business goal (expressed quantitatively)	Boost profit by increasing the number of sales in the store
KPI (key performance indicator)	Number of daily customers who visit the store and make a purchase
Measurement (before) (where we are currently, using our KPI)	Average of 50 customers a day in the past month
Leap (What digital marketing activity are we going to try? How are we going to do it?)	Create a series of Facebook ads that are geo-targeted (meaning, they will only be shown to people within a certain geographic distance of the store). The ads will say "Get Directions" at the bottom, so when people click the ad, they will receive directions to the store. We will track the number of people who viewed and clicked the ad (through Facebook's advertising reports) and the number of customers who make a purchase in the store daily (through the store's point-of-sale system).
Measurement (after) (where we are after, using our KPI)	The number of people who viewed the Facebook ad was just over 1,200, and 187 people clicked it. The health food store saw an average of 55 customers a day (in the store) during the run of the Facebook ad campaign.
Learn (How did you do? What have you learned? What would you do differently next time?)	During the run of the Facebook ad campaign, we saw a 10 percent increase in customers making purchases in the store. Next time, we'll change the Facebook ad to include a special promotion. That might entice even more customers to come to the store.

Spin the wheel again

After the first phase of the digital marketing framework, you can use it again. But this time you go through the framework, it's no longer a series of steps. It's an iterative cycle, and it looks like this:

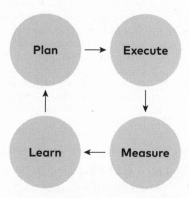

In chart form, it looks like this (continuing with the example from the health food store).

Plan (What are you going to do? How does it serve your business goal? What KPI are you watching for?)	Based on what we learned in the first digital marketing campaign, we will do another round of Facebook ads to entice even more customers to the store. This time, instead of having the ad click go to directions to the store, the ad click will go to a special promotion. This will hopefully bring in more people to the store, which serves our business goal of boosting profit by increasing the number of sales. We're going to keep an eye on the KPI (number of sales), which is currently 55 per day.
Execute (What are the details of the digital marketing campaign?)	As before, we'll create Facebook ads that only display to people who are geographically close to the store. People who click on the ad will be taken to a special page of our website with a promo coupon. Customers can show the coupon in store (on their smartphones) to redeem it.

Measure (How did you do?)	We tracked the number of people who clicked the Facebook ads, the number of people who redeemed the coupon in store, and the most important metric: the number of customer purchases daily. That increased from 55 to 70.
Learn (What have you learned? What would you do differently next time?)	We saw a 27 percent increase in daily sales at the store during the time that the Facebook ads were running. Surprisingly, only three to four people a day showed the coupon at checkout. Anecdotally, the cashier staff mentioned that a few people said they saw the coupon but forgot it. That doesn't matter in the end, though. The Facebook ad campaign was successful because it fulfilled our business goal: boosting profits through increased sales in the store.

In this new cycle, the Leap phase is replaced by a Plan phase. It's no longer a leap because you have some experience to draw on now. Learn from that experience and use it to plan the next phase. When you're planning, don't forget to set your KPI—what you'll measure in this cycle. It might be the same as the last cycle, or it might be a new KPI. Either is fine; what's important is noting what you're going to watch for and which metric you'll keep your eye on as you move through the cycle.

Then execute the plan. Measure. Learn. Wash, rinse, repeat.

Sounds simple enough, right? Hold on to your hats, because in practice, it's anything but. In this book, you'll see a few Caution sections. These are areas where people often deviate from the Goal > Plan > Execute > Measure > Learn cycle. Learn from others' mistakes, so you can stay on the path.

What happens if you skip the process?

One of the first caution moments I want to call out is when people skip the first few steps of the framework. This happened to Leena, a real estate broker. Here's her story.

LEENA IS AN early adopter of new digital marketing tools, particularly social media. She enjoys spending time on her smartphone, posting to Twitter, Facebook, and Instagram when she's out at open houses or in the few minutes she often has between client meetings and property showings. At a networking event for small business owners in her city, Leena heard about a new social media platform called Ello. According to the people Leena was talking with, Ello was supposed to be as good as Facebook but ad-free, and apparently *everyone* was signing up. Leena couldn't believe that she hadn't heard of Ello and that she didn't have an account yet.

Leena was sure that being one of the first people on a new social media platform would be huge for her business, and she needed to get on it right away. Driven by FOMO (the fear of missing out), Leena signed up for an Ello account that evening.

She looked for connections on the platform but could only find a handful of people she knew. *Must be because it's new*, she thought. Leena posted on Ello daily for a few weeks, trying to drum up interest in a hot, new loft property her brokerage had exclusive access to. There were a few comments on her posts, but Leena struggled to find the kind of quality, local connections on Ello that she had on other social media platforms. She couldn't see any correlation between her activity on Ello and inquiries about the loft, or any other properties she had listed. Leena started to spend less and less time on the platform, and within two months of signing up, Leena stopped using Ello altogether.

————————————

IF LEENA'S STORY sounds familiar to you, that's because it's so common. I see it all the time. People jump on a digital marketing tool or social media platform because it's new and shiny, and they don't want to be left behind. Leena skipped the steps of Goal and Plan, running headfirst into the Execute phase. The initial excitement of a new tool wore off fast (it always does), and before long, something that seemed fun at first became a chore. Posting to Ello was yet another thing on Leena's long to-do list. No wonder she jumped ship: it wasn't working for her, and it was a waste of time.

If you start using a digital tool before you know what you want to achieve with it, and before you make a plan for getting you closer to that goal, you'll waste your time just like Leena did.

Because here's the thing: digital marketing is hard. At some point, I promise you, it will feel like a slog. When you're tired and you have to drum up the energy to update the content on your website to be Google-friendly. Or when it's long past quittin' time and you'd much rather close your laptop than create the email newsletter that's supposed to go out in the morning.

Every small business owner I've ever worked with feels the pressure of limited time and resources. You're constantly trying to weigh the effort of any marketing initiative in your business against the potential reward it will bring. And if you're not sure it *is* going to bring you a reward, it can be so tempting to skip it. This is why you can't blow past any of the steps in this process. When the going gets tough, you have to be able to measure (and confidently know) if the juice is worth the squeeze. And if it's not, then it's totally okay to move on to something else! The important part is *knowing*. That's what the framework is for. When you work through the steps of Goal > Plan > Execute > Measure > Learn, in order, you'll be able to confidently say what's working, what's not, and where to go next.

FROM 30,000 FEET TO THE WEEDS... AND BACK

If you own or work for a small business, you're probably really good at quickly shifting from the view at 30,000 feet to being down in the weeds, and back again. In small businesses, there aren't people who are solely thinkers and other people who are solely doers. The tasks of strategy and execution are often carried out by the same person, who can nimbly switch between seeing the plan and moving on it.

In the next few chapters of this book, we're going to get down into the weeds. We're going to go through the particulars of the tech stuff you need to know to build your business online. You will likely feel tempted to look up and try to see the big view. Lean in to this instinct! Keep the digital marketing framework in the back of your mind, even as you're in the trenches, and always be asking, "How does this tie back to my business goal?" It's the prize, and if you keep your eye on it, I can pretty much guarantee you'll be successful.

Grab hold of that business goal, keep it top of mind, and let's dig in.

2

Domain Names, Email, and Hosting

KATE RUNS A small but mighty flower business in her mid-sized city. She has a cute storefront on one of the busiest streets in town, and she attracts a lot of foot traffic. The store windows probably have something to do with it: her gorgeous floral displays are irresistible to passersby. Kate doesn't have a strong online presence for her flower shop, mostly because she's so busy building bouquets that she's not in front of her computer much. She doesn't have a website for her flower store, but she does have an Instagram account where she shares photos of the blooms that head out the door with happy customers.

When the local newspaper wanted to profile Kate and her popular store for Valentine's Day (one of the biggest days of the year for her), she was thrilled to participate. But when the feature came out, Kate noticed something. All of the other businesses profiled included URLs that matched their business names. All Kate had was a link to her Instagram and a Hotmail email account for people to get in touch. She realized that it looked unprofessional and didn't represent her brand well. Kate needed to up her game online, so her digital presence would match the high calibre of her offline business.

———

LIKE KATE, YOU need a web presence that reflects who you are and what you have to say. You need a place to direct your followers to your services, your live events, or your new products, where it's easy to get in touch with you.

But before we even talk about designing your actual web presence (that's in the next chapter), let's dig into the basics. Getting set up like a boss means that you need to learn about domain names, websites, and email. These are the foundation upon which you'll build your digital empire. You can't futureproof your entire business, but you can plan for scaling your aims over time.

What's in a domain name?

You're already familiar with domain names: they're the address of a website or the end of an email address. You know what I'm talking about, because they all end in .com, .ca, .net, .org, and many other fun endings like .info or .car. Examples include Wikipedia.org, NYTimes.com, or my own CampTech.ca and AverySwartz.com. In my experience, domain names and how they work, how they integrate with email and website hosting, are an area of confusion for a lot of people. But once you understand the logic behind them, you'll be ready to rock.

THE COLLECTOR

SOME WOMEN COLLECT shoes. I collect domain names. Or, at least, I used to.

As an entrepreneur, I have had a fair amount of *Oh wow, that would be a great idea for a business* moments. And when I felt that rush of a new business idea, I often registered a domain name for the imaginary business I might start.

I don't do it so much anymore, since I'm so focused on Camp Tech these days, but I do still own a bunch of domain names for my past business ideas. Many I'll let go, but some I'll keep holding on to—they're still good ideas and I just might launch them someday. A fun example comes from a business idea I had with my husband. We thought we'd start a podcast where we'd discuss two topics we love: craft beer brewing (him) and the internet (me). They intersect more than you'd think! We were going to call the podcast *Craft and Code*, so I registered CraftAndCode.ca right away, so the show would have a home online. We still haven't made the podcast, but I'm holding on to the domain name in case we do.

How the sausage gets made

How does this all work? Everything connected to the internet is given an identifier called an Internet Protocol address (IP address). An IP address is a string of numbers (like 205.186.179.111) that identifies a specific location on a computer or group of computers connected to the internet. Every website, computer, smartphone, internet-enabled refrigerator, artificial intelligence home device like Alexa or Google Home—every single one of these has an IP address. The internet is a pretty busy place with lots of things going on, so every piece of it needs a unique identifier or things could get really messy. The computers that connect the different parts of the internet together reference each other by IP address.

But we're humans, not robots. Words are much easier for us to remember than a string of numbers. So, we use domain names, so we don't have to remember IP addresses. Because we're not likely to say to our friends at the office, "Hey! Did you see the top story on 199.198.138.49 this morning?" But we might say, "Hey! Did you see the top story on GlobeAnd Mail.com this morning?"

When you type a domain name into your web browser, it quickly checks to see if that domain name is linked to a particular IP address, and then it takes you to that place on the internet. How does this work? Your web browser taps into the domain name system (DNS), which is like a giant switchboard connecting domain names to IP addresses for websites and email processing.

You have to have a few checks and balances in place to make sure that everything works smoothly.

Registering domain names

You can't add a domain name to the DNS yourself. You have to get into the system through a *registrar*, which is a company that registers domain names on your behalf. The most commonly known domain name registrar is GoDaddy. They're a fine one, although they're not my preferred registrar. I register my domain names at Hover.com because I like their customer service.

When you register a domain name, you are the *registrant*, and the registration company is the *registrar*. Most registrars have access to the domain name extensions I've mentioned (.com, .info, .net, .org) and you get to pick what goes to the left of the dot, as long as it's not already taken. Some registrars also have access to country-specific domain name extensions like .ca for Canada, .mx for Mexico, .is for Iceland, and so on, which are intended to be associated with citizens, organizations, or businesses in those specific locations. In 2012, the Internet Corporation for Assigned Names and Numbers (ICANN) opened up a bidding process to allow more domain name extensions (also known as "top-level domain extensions" or TLDs) and more than 600 were purchased. Many of them are available through domain registrars now, so you can knock yourself out and register your own .pizza, .party, .school, .taxi, .yoga domain, and many more.

What's important to know is that, other than the branding and marketing possibilities that come with choosing a domain name extension, there are no actual technical differences between them. Google and other search engines don't have a preference for particular domain extensions, so choose the one that best suits your business or organizational intentions. If the exact same website was launched at Avery Swartz.com and AverySwartz.pizza, for example, Google won't rank one higher than the other in search engine results. What does matter is that AverySwartz.com makes much more sense as my primary website for my marketing efforts. If I end up expanding my brand to include pizza or yoga or any other aim, then I could consider adding another domain—you're allowed to purchase as many as you want.

My suggestion? Buy a bunch of domain names that represent your current business name. They're not super expensive (depending on the domain extension, registration is usually around $15 to $20 a year). That way you don't have to pick between a .com or a .ca. If both are available, buy both. There is some method to the madness of buying more than one domain name if multiple domain name extensions are available. If you own a domain name, then no one else can buy it.

I worked with a children's book author once who wanted to register her own name as her domain name. We were able to register the .ca version of her name, and since she's based in Canada, that worked well. We couldn't get the .com version of her name because it was being used already... by an adult film star! Talk about confusion in the marketplace. My client wished she had purchased the .com version of her name years ago, so no one else could.

That being said, you don't need to go wild registering domain names. One company I worked with took my advice a little too far: they registered more than 80 different iterations of their business name. That was definitely going overboard (not to mention expensive!). Bottom line: grab one main domain name, and if there are any that are similar (including easy and likely mistakes people could make), grab those too.

There are some important things that you need to know when registering your domain, whichever one(s) you choose.

1   You *can* register a domain name and not do anything with it. It can just sit there.

2   You *should* register your domain name yourself, instead of getting your web person to do it for you. It's important that your name is listed as the registrant for the domain, because that means you're the legal owner. Proving ownership can be a real headache if, in the future you want to change domain name registrars or make any changes to the registration, such as your contact information.

3   You *can't* buy a domain name that's already registered, unless someone is willing to sell it. To find out the registrant of a domain name, you can do a Whois search (whois.com/whois). Sometimes you'll see the actual person's name and address listed; sometimes you'll see the name of the registration company if the registrant chose not to make their Whois information public. If you're trying to get in touch with them, you can email the registration company, but think twice before trying to buy an already-owned domain. It's usually not worth the hassle. People selling domains can be pretty shady. I don't recommend doing it yourself; get a good broker to do it for you and take care of your interests in the process.

4   You *can* point several domain names to the same website. For example, think about my name: Avery Swartz. Not Schwartz. It's misspelled all the time, so I registered the domain names AverySwartz.com, AverySwartz.ca, Avery Schwartz.com, and AverySchwartz.ca and all of them point to one website. We'll get into how this works in the Hosting section below.

5   Always *remember* that your domain name has to be renewed. You need to ensure that you auto-renew your

name *and* that your credit card information for this service is up-to-date.

That's pretty much it. Once you have your domain name sorted out, you can create unique email addresses, build and host a website, and do everything else you need to do to manage your business online, one step at a time.

CAUTION! WRITE IT DOWN

IT SOUNDS OBVIOUS, but keeping up-to-date records of your domain name registration, website hosting, email services, and any other technical account info is so important. One of my clients, Louisa, an accountant, got herself into real trouble with this.

Here's what happened. Louisa had asked her administrator, Stephen, to do the domain name registration for the accounting firm's website. Stephen put Louisa's name as the registrar for the domain name but his own work email as the contact on the account. Stephen set the domain name to auto-renew annually, and they were off to the races. A few years later, Stephen moved on from the company and his email account was shut down. Around the same time, the domain name was up for renewal, but it couldn't auto-renew because the credit card on file had expired. No one had updated the contact information on file at the domain registration company, so all the emails they sent Louisa's business weren't getting through (because Stephen's email address had been closed). With no updated credit card number, and no response to the emails they were sending, the domain registration company didn't renew Louisa's business's domain name. That caused the website to go down.

Luckily, Louisa noticed quickly that her website wasn't working, so she reached out to the domain registration company. They explained that they had been trying to get in touch with her and that they needed an updated credit card number to renew the domain. Louisa gave that to them, updated the contact info on the account, and learned her lesson to always keep her records up-to-date!

Hosting your website

Once you have your primary domain registered, you have to create a link between that and the website itself, namely the pictures, data, and words that you want to share online. No, we haven't talked about creating the website yet, but that's because you need a place to build it. If your website is your home, your hosting location is an empty property, ready for you to build whatever you want, when you want.

Sometimes domain name registrars will also offer hosting packages and wrap everything up in a neat little bundle: domain name registration, website hosting, and email hosting (we'll get to that in a moment) all in one place. If that works for you, go for it. You can bundle everything together, or get your domain name registration, website hosting, and email solution separately. Explore your options first to make sure you know what you want, and if you can get it all in one place, fine. If not, buy them all from different providers.

Depending on what kind of website you're going to have, you may not even need to arrange for your own website hosting. Some website builder platforms, like Squarespace and Shopify, provide website hosting for you as part of their monthly fee. There's more about this in the next chapter.

Most hosting packages will be *managed*. What this means is that these hosting companies will provide you with direct technical services such as website and software setup and configuration, maintenance, technical support, updating, and monitoring for you. Most of these services (but not all) can even return your website to a previous state if the site crashes or is hacked, so that you don't lose your site or its data.

Email on all the things

When you have a domain name, you can create email addresses using that name (e.g., yourname@yourdomain.com), which looks way more professional than a generic email address from Hotmail or Gmail. If you want email associated with your domain name, then you need your email hosted somewhere.

Nope, email hosting is not the same as website hosting. They're similar but technically different. In fact, whether you have a website or not, you can have a domain name for email (as long as you own that domain name, of course). Remember a domain name is just an address to a place—it's not a place itself. Domain names point web stuff to websites (hosted on web servers) and email stuff to email servers (hosted on mail servers).

Sometimes, when you get a web hosting package, an email solution is included. Unless it's one of the two I recommend below, it's likely not a great option. A lot of website hosting companies offer simple email software that sounds okay, but in practice it's a pain to use. You might end up having to deal with delayed or failed email delivery, bouncing sent messages, or lots of spam. Skip the free stuff and go with an email solution from an industry leader: Google or Microsoft.

Google's email hosting solution, **G Suite**, might be the best way to rid yourself of spam. I'm sure you know about Gmail, but what you may not know is that you can host your own domain name email through Google's servers. This means you can use Gmail but with your own, branded email address (yourname@yourdomain.com), instead of a Gmail email address (yourcompanyname@gmail.com). There are good reasons why you may want to consider this option: for one thing, it can be relatively inexpensive and easy to access online; for another, Google has one of the best spam filters in the world. When you're managing hundreds of emails a day, knowing that you will rarely have to deal with spam is a relief.

Microsoft's solution, **Office 365**, may work for you if you plan to integrate your email with other Office 365 software applications for admin or management reasons. You've probably used MS Outlook if you've worked in an office at some point in your life. You can use Outlook with your own branded email address and access it from anywhere (on any device, via the Outlook app or a web browser). If you're already familiar with Microsoft Office or MS Outlook, stick with what you know and use Microsoft's solution for hosted email.

Whether you choose Google's or Microsoft's email solution, the first step is to create an account with them. There will be a monthly fee, but it's nominal. Then you need to "point" your domain name to them so your email will be sent through. This sounds technical, and it kind of is, but remember you're one of many, many people who do this. It's a common request for a domain name registrar to point email to Google's or Microsoft's mail servers. Ask your domain name registration company to help you—customer service is part of what you're paying for!

Speaking of email addresses, let's talk briefly about how they should look.

A lot of people love using yourfirstname@yourbizname .com (e.g., avery@camptech.ca). It's a solid choice: it's accessible and often easiest to remember. But here's the catch: if your business grows, what if you hire someone else with the same first name? Will you add their last initial? A number? Change the system entirely? Whatever you want to do is fine, but if naming consistency is important to you, you may want to consider another option. A safer choice is yourfirst namelastinitial@yourbizname.com (averys@camptech.ca), or something else entirely. Companies regularly choose options like firstnamelastname@ (averyswartz@camptech .ca), firstname.lastname@ (avery.swartz@camptech.ca), or firstinitiallastname@ (aswartz@camptech.ca) to make things consistent, but there's nothing wrong with being more creative, if it suits your industry (e.g., nerd@camptech.ca). Pick a system and stick with it.

CHAPTER 2 FROM 30,000 FEET

Register a domain name that matches the name of your business.

→ Do this through a registrar (a domain name registration company).
→ Consider registering more than one domain name.
→ Make sure you register your domain names yourself—your name needs to be on the registration documentation.

You may or may not need to source your own website hosting, depending on what kind of website you're going to have.

You can order domain name registration, website hosting, and email all from the same company or separately.

You need email hosting to use your domain name for an email address (such as yourname@yourcompany.com).

→ Email hosting is sometimes included in website hosting packages, but it's often a bare-bones solution.
→ Email solutions from Google and Microsoft are the most robust.

3

Yes, You Need a Website

I F A CUSTOMER googles a business and no website turns up, does it even exist?

Okay, that's a bratty question. But you get where I'm going with it. Christian is an independent insurance broker and financial planner. He's been in business for 25 years and has never had a website. Most of Christian's clients find him using the best form of marketing there is: word of mouth. His current clients refer him to new clients; for the most part, that works well for Christian. He even sends thank-you gifts to his clients to reward them for the referrals. He doesn't think he needs a website because he gets enough business through word-of-mouth marketing. But in the last few years, he's noticed something—people are actually asking for him to have a website! Christian's current clients have told him it would be easier to refer him if they had a link to share. They know that a website brings credibility to a business, and even though their friends and family trust their referral, a site to look at makes the likelihood that they'll reach out to Christian stronger.

EVEN IF YOU'VE been in business for a long time like Christian, not having a website is sort of like not having a phone number. A website is the only thing that works everywhere— because the web is everywhere. From desktops to laptops to smartphones to tablets to televisions, devices that connect to the internet have a web browser.

The easiest way to reach your audience is to create a website as a central platform for everything you want to do. You can use your website to share information about your services, sell your products, create a sense of connection with your clients, or build a community. It's an important investment for your future work. You need a website designed to grow with you and allow you to take advantage of every opportunity. It needs to appeal to your current and prospective clients and customers.

And social media isn't, or shouldn't be, a replacement for your own site.

Let's start with the fact that a website is yours, and you control its future based on your business goals and decisions. Social media platforms aren't yours. In fact, as we are learning more and more lately, the companies that do own them have their own plans for the platforms that may or likely may not align with your own.

Anyone who has managed a Facebook business page over the last few years knows what it feels like to be at the whim of a changeable master. Every time Facebook makes a change to the way its users can interact with the platform, there are repercussions for people using the service to try to reach others. You're constantly rolling with the punches, having to adapt to change that you didn't ask for. And remember Myspace? In its heyday, Myspace was wildly popular and some businesses decided to build the core of their digital presence on it. But where is Myspace now? It still exists, but it would be laughable to encourage your customers or clients to visit your business's home on the internet by going to a Myspace page.

Why build your castle on someone else's land?

I'm not suggesting you shouldn't have social media profiles. You most certainly can and should (and I'll tell you more about them in chapter 8). The internet moves fast and is unpredictable. It's not unlike a marketplace. I don't know much about the stock market, but I do know that a sound investing strategy is to diversify your portfolio of investments in a variety of holdings. The same holds true here: don't put all your digital eggs in one basket. Spread 'em out a bit. But keep the most important part of your digital strategy— your home base—as your own website.

Planning and measuring website success

How will you know if your website is successful or not? Before we get into the nuts and bolts of how to actually build a website, let's talk about setting yourself up for success. For many of the small business owners I work with, having and maintaining a website is a pain. They know and agree that they need one (they are my clients after all, and I've told them everything I just told you about why websites are essential business tools). But websites are often seen as just a necessary expense. Some people think of them as being the modern version of business cards—they're something you just *have to have*, and they cost money, not make it.

I encourage you to challenge this way of thinking. If a website is planned and executed properly, it won't only be an expense—it'll be an asset. Just like I taught you in chapter 1, keep your business goal in mind when planning your website and identify your key performance indicator (KPI) before you get started.

How will you know if your website is succeeding? If your website is an online store and your KPI is a very direct and easily measured metric (like online sales volume), then you should be able to tell fairly quickly if your website is doing its job. But what if you're not in an ecommerce business? What if your website is purely informational? You can still pick a KPI to measure success. Metrics like the length of time someone spends on your website and the number of pages they view in a single website visit can indicate whether they're engaged with your site's content. If you have a contact form that can be filled out, an email signup button that can be clicked, or some other sort of content where an action can be taken, it can be measured.

It's time for some real talk, friends. Making a website is a major undertaking, especially if you're going to do it yourself. But even if you hire a pro to help, you still have to be involved in the process. Working on a website will take you away from your actual work for at least a few weeks, if not longer. While I hope you enjoy the process of building your web presence, the truth is that a lot of people don't.

This is why it's essential to think about how you're going to quantifiably measure your website success now, at the planning stage. This will help you keep your eye on the prize and remember why you're going through the pain of making a website (or the expense of having one made for you). When the going gets tough (and I promise you, it *will* get tough), you'll know why you're making the darn thing in the first place.

Hiring someone to make your website

The first big question when you're building a website is: should you do it yourself or should you hire someone to make it for you? Let's start by looking at what's involved in hiring someone else.

First, you need to understand the difference between a website *designer* and a website *developer*. These are two entirely different sets of professional skills.

- **Designers** create the visual style and content of the site, such as decisions around layout, colours, fonts, photography, graphics, and video.

- **Developers** are the people who code the site and adapt software to your specific needs.

Some people do both of these things, and some specialize. User experience designers, for example, are specialists in how people engage with the website, how much time they spend in certain areas, and whether people are using the features of the site in expected or unexpected ways. Some developers focus on online stores or customer database development.

Whether you work with a designer or a developer or both, the process is all about effective communication.

Alright, Avery, of course I have to communicate well, you're thinking. *That's a given.*

It may be a given, but here's a big thing: while you're hiring someone to help you out, you're also new at this. That means that you have to be able to ask a lot of questions, and you have to listen carefully. This process is likely going to be a lot different from hiring, say, another professional service provider like a plumber or even from choosing art for your home. A plumber has one job: to make the pipes work perfectly. A piece of art also has one job: to please you. A designer/ developer has multiple jobs: to please you, to make things work perfectly, and, most importantly, *to please your clients*.

You see, your website is not about you.

Okay, maybe it is about you, but the fact is that you're not building your website to put on your wall and admire it. You're building it to sell products or share information about your services. To do that, *your website has to work for other people more than it works for you*.

Great web design should do a few things well:

- create a seamless and easy experience for people who go to your website so that they can find what they are looking for;

- ensure that people do what you want them to do (buy something, register for a course, read about the work you do, book a consulting session), both in the short and long term; and

- represent your brand and values clearly.

The best websites achieve these goals in a seemingly effortless way. Over the years of working on websites with my clients, the most common request I've received is "I want it to feel like Apple's website." That's not because my clients want to rip off Apple's brand—it's because they inherently understand that clean, clear design creates a wonderful website visiting experience.

You can create a similar experience for your website visitors through the use of website *conventions*. Your web designer and developer will know these—they're the specific things that make it easier for people to navigate your site.

Website conventions include things like placing the search box in the upper right-hand corner, your logo in the upper left-hand corner, and the navigation menu somewhere at the top (either centred or to the side), and so forth. These are the places that people generally look for information. If they can't find this information quickly, they are likely to get frustrated and search elsewhere.

When you have your first meeting with a designer, start with listening to their ideas for how to engage your clients. Don't naturally lean back into your own visual ideals, because creating a top-notch user experience is not the same as creating the perfect living room. They will know what it takes to get your client in the door, purchase your products, and book your services, and what visual cues are necessary to make that happen. The same goes with developers. They've built websites before and will have insight into what tech functionality is considered best practice.

This is not to say that you don't have any choices in the matter. Your website is about your company, and, of course, you'll want your imprint on it. But start with flexibility and an open mind—and the following questions.

10 important questions to ask developers and designers

There are some questions you should ask a web professional before you get them to design or build a website for you.

1   **How long have you been in the business?** It's important to understand how much experience someone has and

what they're able to bring to the table. You might want to ask the developer or designer to show you samples of their recent work.

2   **What web platforms do you use?** There are very few developers or designers who code websites completely from scratch these days. If they do, it might end up costing you a lot more, not only right away but down the road every time you need an update. If they use WordPress or Squarespace, for example, you'll be able to update your text and drop pictures in after the core site is built, but if they use a system that's unknown or one they've created themselves, you may have to pay for every change.

3   **What's your style?** Look at the professional portfolio they're offering. Is it all splashes of neon yellow and glittery logos that make you roll your eyes? Is it all muted tones and boring boxes? A good designer can adapt to a range of styles while still keeping to conventions that work for everyone. This isn't about judging the style of other company's brands and websites. You're looking to see if the designer is a one-trick pony. Is there diversity in style, and does each style represent the brand it's associated with? Or is it all one similar look? If all the websites that person makes look the same, then don't expect yours will be any different.

4   **How proficient are you at making changes to website templates?** Web platforms often come with pre-made templates for webpages, but these can be changed and restyled by developers or designers. If you want a specific look and feel for your site, you want to know that your

developer or designer can handle the task of template customization. Ask them to show you samples.

5   **Do you need any extra technical help? Can you set up the database and server for me, or do we need to bring in someone else here?** Your developer or designer will have to upload your site to a server (see the Hosting section in chapter 2). If they're comfortable doing this, it can save you a lot of hassle. Find out how much they charge for server adjustments in the future, so that you can compare this to the services provided by your hosting company. If you have a customer mailing list that is collected on your website, your developer or designer will have to integrate a database, usually using third-party software. Simple databases are free to install in most web platform environments using plugins, widgets, or in the template itself, but there may be some technical configuration necessary.

6   **What happens in an emergency, and what's your plan for ongoing maintenance?** If you're hacked, is this person going to help you recover your site? Do they have regular support hours, when you can actually reach them? What's their response time in a support situation? If they aren't going to be the person who helps you with ongoing site maintenance, you need to know ahead of time so that you have a contingency plan in place, and you know who (and who not) to call. Ask for their recommendations for backup plans. Some website platforms, like WordPress, need technical maintenance. Who's gonna do that? You? Will you be trained?

7   **Are there other skills you bring to the table?** Is your designer or developer experienced in traditional marketing? Public relations? Writing and editing? Video production? What benefits might they be able to add, especially for jobs that you don't feel confident doing yourself?

8   **What's your process for developing a website?** There's no right answer for this one, but designers and developers who have experience will know their website process like the back of their hand and will recite it from memory, which makes things easier and, eventually, less expensive. It's important for you to find out how it's going to work if you proceed with this professional, and vet if they're a great match for you and your goals. For example, creating mock-ups of the designs usually involves two, or sometimes three, revisions before everyone is happy. You shouldn't expect your professional to do endless revisions of designs or the site itself. Ask how many revisions are included in the price and what the extra charge is for going over.

9   **How do you test the website once it's built?** Does the designer or developer rely on their own instincts, or do they go through a rigorous user testing process? What does that look like? What about technical testing for bugs? Does the designer or developer have a technical QA (quality assurance) checklist?

10 **When will you be able to get started?** If the answer is "today," that's not a great sign. Most web professionals who are busy (and in demand because they are good at their jobs) will be able to fit you into their docket a few weeks after an initial meeting.

Check those references

Looking through someone's portfolio of work is a great way to see what they can do. But it only shows the end result—it doesn't show how they got there. What was the process like? Agonizing? Awesome? The only way to know what your working relationship might be like is to get in touch with people who have worked with this professional before. Ask for references and actually contact them to ask what it was like to work with this person—before you sign a contract. Oh, and while we're on that subject, please don't forget to have a contract with your web professional, okay? Have a lawyer look at it too, especially any section pertaining to ownership of designs, code, or intellectual property.

How much should your website cost?

Ah, the fundamental question.

The challenge that a lot of designers face these days is that there are many new overseas shops that provide websites on the cheap. But why have a terrible design created by a developer alone (rather than someone with user experience design skills), without user testing, no exciting features, and nothing innovative? Not to mention what a headache it can be to work with someone who's trying to do everything on the cheap. The service you receive will be subpar, and you likely won't be able to make revisions.

All this is to say that, as with many things, you get what you pay for. If you are looking to hire a designer or development firm, don't necessarily go for the cheapest rate. Most website professionals will talk with you about your needs and provide an estimate free of charge, so it's worth shopping around a bit.

The price of a website can vary wildly. I once advised a client who had received multiple estimates for a website redesign, ranging from $18,000 to $130,000! The price often depends on how much design work is needed, how the site is built (technically), and how fast you need it done.

Consider: do you need only an information website, or do you want to add a store, a video centre, an online training module, or more? All of these components add to the complexity of what you are asking for—and the cost.

A good place to start to build your plans and budget is How Much Does a Website Cost (howmuchdoesawebsiteco.st). This site can provide you with a basic estimate of what you should expect to pay a designer or developer or both for your new home on the web, so that you don't get sticker shock right out of the gate.

Creating your own website

What if your website needs are simple? You can most definitely create your website yourself. Especially if all you need, right out of the gate, is a *landing page*—that's tech-speak for a simple single-page marketing website that gets your message across. Landing pages are designed for a single purpose: to announce a new product that's coming soon, to get people to sign up for your newsletter, to provide background information on what you do and who works on your team, or to develop any business conversion goal. A website homepage is a type of landing page and may act as a portal to many different aspects of the website.

Here's the great part: there are many different easy-to-use website platforms that can help you build a landing page or site in minutes, even without a web designer. Web builder tools like Squarespace and WordPress.com, for example, can help you create a simple but very effective landing page, and Shopify can help you create an online store. Some of these tools will provide you with free or low-cost hosting as well: you can choose from many different options to get started and then build your web presence over time. Some of these platforms even allow you to literally drag and drop your materials into a live website and keep your content updated yourself. For this reason, many web platforms are also called content management systems (CMS). If you can use Microsoft Word or compose an email with basic formatting, you'll be able to use a CMS to keep your website up-to-date on your own.

No matter what platform you use, you're going to need a responsive (mobile-friendly) template with a modern design that's easy to navigate. You want the design to help you do two primary things:

1   get people to information they need easily, and
2   ensure that the site is optimized to be viewed on all digital devices (through responsive design, which we'll cover in the next chapter).

WordPress and Squarespace, which are primarily suited to marketing websites, and Shopify, suited to online store websites, can achieve these goals. There are other web platforms out there too, including Wix, Weebly, GoDaddy Website Builder, BigCommerce, and more. I particularly like WordPress, Squarespace, and Shopify for small businesses, though, for reasons I'll tell you about.

WordPress

WordPress takes some work to get started, but it opens you up to a wide range of growing features that ensure your technology does not become dated. For many businesses, the beauty of WordPress is in its scalability: it can grow as your business grows. Its benefits are clear, in that the setup process is well developed (you'll find lots of online resources to help with any problem you face) and it's straightforward to manage, but it requires some commitment to get going.

WordPress is one of the world's most widely used website building software systems. There are two versions of WordPress: WordPress.org (also known as "self-hosted WordPress") and WordPress.com. The choice between these options largely depends on the level of control you want over the design, functionality, and management of your website.

This table lays it all out for you.

	WordPress.org (self-hosted)	WordPress.com
Version	The full version of the WordPress software with all of its bells and whistles.	A light version of WordPress that includes only basic functions.
Hosting	You have to provide hosting yourself.	Hosted for you on a free plan, with the option to upgrade to a paid plan for more features.
Domain name	You need to get (and pay for) your own.	Unless you upgrade to a paid plan that includes a custom domain name, a WordPress.com site will always have the extension "wordpress.com" in the site name.
Ease of use	More complex; learning some coding tools can make a difference.	Instant ease—no coding expertise needed.

	WordPress.org (self-hosted)	WordPress.com
Control	It's like owning a house: you can do whatever you want, but you're responsible for any problems you cause. It's up to you, the website owner, to maintain the site, aside from features offered by the hosting provider, and to install the plugins and other elements for customizing the site.	It's like renting: you have some control but not all. But since it's a controlled environment, you have someone to turn to if something breaks.
Options	All options depend on what the site owner needs; a collection of templates that can be modified are included, and you can download others for a fee.	Personal, Premium, and Business packages are available for a fee.
Functionality	You can add plugins for any function you need, like online stores, databases, or video pages.	No plugins allowed, unless you pay for a plan that includes them.
Content	You can easily add content by typing it in directly or copying and pasting from somewhere else.	You can easily add content by typing it in directly or copying and pasting from somewhere else.
Best for...	People who have businesses or organizations that are likely to grow fast or need functionality beyond simple words and images.	Students, bloggers, and creatives who don't have a need for—or interest in—the full range of customization options.

So, to sum up, it's worth it to consider a WordPress site for three major reasons.

1   It's the most scalable solution out there, which means that it can grow with you no matter what you want to do with your website.

2   You can set it up with or without professional help, which means that you can start or finish a WordPress site yourself and learn as you go.

3   It's open-source software, which means you don't need to pay a licensing fee to a company to use it. It can be modified and shared and hosted anywhere.

Squarespace

Squarespace is a bit of a different animal, one that many people find much easier to use than WordPress. It's great for information websites and landing pages, because you can pick out a template and customize it with your content as easily as you would fill out a web form. It's a system created with the novice in mind, and the company does what it does very well: provide beautiful and easy systems that almost anyone would feel comfortable using. The site is hosted for you by Squarespace (part of your monthly fee) and you can use your own domain name.

Why *wouldn't* you pick Squarespace? It's not the greatest solution for the long term, unless you simply need a digital brochure. For many companies and organizations, that's fine! A Squarespace site is a lightweight solution, and there's nothing wrong with that. The challenge is that if and when you grow your business, you may outgrow your Squarespace site. And that's okay as well. If you grow so much that you need to invest in a new site, then that's a great problem to have.

Shopify

What if you want a plug-and-play website, but your focus is selling products online? That's where Shopify might be your best solution. As easy to use as other tools but with a greater set of resources for online stores, Shopify also allows you to pick out a template and customize it with your content. Shopify hosts the website on their servers (again, part of the monthly fee as with Squarespace) and you can use your own domain name for your online store. Shopify also has a point-of-sale solution and Facebook and Instagram selling capacity, which means that you're going to be ready to build your sales strategy across a number of different platforms right away.

But there's more you need to know if you're planning to sell stuff online.

Selling stuff online

If you're going to engage in ecommerce, you have some decisions to make: how to sell, how to get paid, and how to keep track of it all.

Where is your store?

Broadly speaking, there are three main ways to sell things online. Let's look at them and explore the pros and cons of each.

Existing site, add-on store. If you already have an information-based website or a blog, you can use a lightweight, add-on ecommerce solution to sell simple items with few options. Think of an author site with books for sale or a website with tickets to an event without reserved seating. Solutions that work for this include adding a section or page to your website using the additions offered by your website platform. WordPress has plugins for stores, and Squarespace's ecommerce add-on package means that you can drag and drop a store into your site. You can also customize any other type of website with a PayPal or Stripe button by following the instructions these companies provide, but you may need help from a developer.

- **Advantages:** You can keep your site rocking while you add on new pages and try new store options. You can also drive your customers to your site through your email promotions (rather than to an online marketplace that may cannibalize your brand).

- **Disadvantages:** You may find that this option is harder to implement than the other two ways to sell stuff online, and it may be more difficult to expand over time unless you pay for a developer's assistance.

External marketplaces: Big-name marketplaces, such as Etsy, which specializes in handmade goods, can be easier to set up than your own site, and they're a great place to test the market before launching your own store. Online marketplaces are great for product discovery too, because they rotate stock and market to your potential customers on your behalf. This means that a customer may have never heard of you before, but they can still discover you through one of Etsy's email campaigns or social media posts. Many people also use Amazon's marketplace for the same reason, but you may be killing your ability to compete against others if you use it, because it tends to attract customers who are only interested in the lowest price. Think carefully and consider all of your options.

- **Advantages:** You can easily add products and promote instantaneously through online marketplaces.

- **Disadvantages:** Paying a cut of sales or a fee is normal for these platforms. Even worse, you don't control the store or where it's aiming its strategy, so if you rely on a marketplace alone, you never know when all of your hard work building in that space will become more expensive or more challenging to manage. Don't build your castle on someone else's land!

Your store *is* your website. You can create a website that is, first and foremost, an online store. Yes, you can add extra stuff like About pages, a Contact page, and even a blog, but the core functionality is as an online shopping experience. This is the best option for selling a variety of products, with product variants (e.g., T-shirts in different styles, colours, and sizes). You can build an online store with solutions like BigCommerce and Magento, but for small businesses, I recommend using Shopify.

- **Advantages:** You can easily add in products, build your online presence, and drive customers to your site, while increasing your ability to expand your brand and strategy over the long term.

- **Disadvantages:** Building an online store takes time and effort. There are a lot of sections to customize (from the product pages all the way to the shipping confirmation messages).

When your store is your website, you're living your strategy as well as creating your online presence. It is the most comprehensive way to engage in building a long-term solution to expanding your company or organization.

What's a payment gateway?

But there's more to it than choosing your platform. When you want to make money, you have to collect it. In the digital world, that means that when you build an online store, you need to select a *payment gateway*. A payment gateway is the financial link between you and your customer. It digitally connects a client's credit card, debit card, or other e-payment to their bank, which connects to your bank, which deposits the money collected in your account. It authorizes the financial transaction for you, acting as a gateway.

When your store is your website, gateway options are usually embedded in the system: some online store builders, such as Shopify, offer their own payment gateway. If they don't have their own, they'll ask you to choose one, like PayPal or Stripe. Your bank may offer its own as well, such as Moneris. The gateways I've listed here are very secure, and they offer support for getting your store connected to your bank. They know what they're doing to get money in the door.

No matter what payment gateway you use, you're going to have to pony up for fees. Some of the bank options may have lower transaction fees but cost you much more to set up, because you may need a developer's help. PayPal may have a higher per-transaction cost, but it is also well supported in terms of ease of setup and management.

The most important thing I can tell you is that before you choose a gateway, compare the fees with the appropriate volume of transactions you're anticipating. There are many different fee structures that change over time, so I'm not going to list them here, but the reality is that you need to look at the small print. Don't skip that step! Read and ask questions. The time to do it is before you set up your store, not after!

What is integration?

In the online world, *integration* is the term most often used for getting two (or more) different digital systems to talk to each other and share information.

Remember my headache with learning new accounting software? A lot of my pain was in figuring out how to properly record Camp Tech's online ticket sales in our accounting books. The trick that made it all work out in the end was an integration. In this case, I connected Camp Tech's Shopify store (where we sell our workshop tickets) to QuickBooks (our accounting software) using a Shopify-to-QuickBooks integration.

When you stick with big-name tech solutions (like QuickBooks or Xero for accounting), there will likely be an integration between that solution and your website. I even recommend checking to see which integrations exist before going too far down the road with any one solution. The best way to check for an integration between two systems is to do a Google search of the names of the pieces you're trying to connect and the word "integration." For example, when I was looking for the Shopify-to-QuickBooks integration for Camp Tech, I literally went to Google and searched for "Shopify QuickBooks integration." That led me to a page on QuickBooks' website explaining how to hook up the two services, so they'd talk to each other.

Some integrations are ready to go right out of the box, and some need configuration. You may even need professional help to get an integration going, but once it's set up, it should "just work" (in theory at least). You simply have to fill in the fields online to make sure that the systems can talk to each other.

Hooking your online store up to your accounting software is only one of many possible integrations you can explore.

Odds are that if you need it for your small business, someone else needs it too and there may be an integration. Here are some of the ecommerce integrations that you may require.

- **Email marketing.** Mailchimp and other email marketing software systems have integrations with most online store solutions, so you can see how your email marketing is driving sales. Connect the dots between your most recent newsletter and the sales of your new product line, and you'll know whether or not your conversion strategies work.

- **Social media.** You can post information about your online store and products to social media yourself, but you can also set an integration to do it for you. There are automatic links between store systems and social media sites that you can set up in advance to advertise new products or services. Social media integrations can also allow your customers to share their purchase info to their social media using a message, hashtag, or handle that you've pre-populated for them, which means that you'll generate positive word of mouth more easily, because you've taken the guesswork out for your customers.

- **Shipping.** You don't want to have to manually look up every order to your online store, write out the address by hand, pack it in your basement, and walk it to the post office, do you? There are a bunch of shipping integrations out there to help, from drop-shipping (getting a fulfillment company to manage your shipping for a nominal fee) to generating shipping labels, to online order tracking with different courier services. Explore the right options for you, depending on where your business or organization is located and what makes sense volume-wise. This is something you can also look at developing over time once you build a following and orders are on the rise!

. . . .

CHAPTER 3 FROM 30,000 FEET

You need a website. Not just word of mouth, and not just social media either—don't build your castle on someone else's land!

. . . .

You can make your website yourself or hire a professional. But if you hire a professional, you need to find out all about them first.

. . . .

In general, with websites, the more you want it to do, the more you have to pay for it.

. . . .

The three best website platforms for small businesses are WordPress, Squarespace, and Shopify:

→ WordPress is scalable, open-source, and has no licensing fees. It has many possibilities if you have the technical resources.
→ Squarespace is great for simple, pretty websites. It's relatively easy to use and fast to set up.
→ Shopify is an online store builder. It can set you up to sell across different platforms.

. . . .

Your three main options for selling things online are adding ecommerce functionality to an existing website, selling through a third-party marketplace like Etsy or Amazon, or building your whole website as an online store with Shopify or a similar provider.

. . . .

Choose your payment gateway wisely: compare fees to the sales volume you realistically expect.

. . . .

Use integrations to hook up your online store to other digital systems, such as accounting, order tracking, or shipping.

. . . .

4

The Three Components of a Modern Website: Mobile, Fast, and Accessible

BRENT AND NISHA are a husband and wife team who own and operate a popular Irish pub. Brent and Nisha knew early on that having a website for their restaurant could be a strong differentiator for them (the restaurant industry has been particularly slow in realizing that websites are an essential part of marketing). They put their first site online in 2006. It was designed and coded for them, using a website technology called Flash that allowed for immersive, interactive websites with animation and sound. The site was expensive to make and hard to maintain, but it perfectly conveyed the experience of dining at their pub.

Flash forward (ba-dum ching) to 2010, when Flash died. Steve Jobs, then CEO of Apple, declared that Flash was a closed-door ecosystem and he didn't want it on Apple products, like the iPhone. Flash still worked for most people viewing the pub's website on a desktop computer, but Brent and Nisha were concerned that people who were "out and about" on their mobile devices wouldn't be able to access it.

They decided to bite the bullet and redesign their site using a different website platform. Brent and Nisha's web designer told them they should consider WordPress, since it featured a content management system that would allow them to update their food and beverage menus and other website content on their own. They launched the new WordPress-powered website for the pub in early 2011.

By 2016, the site was starting to show cracks. Brent and Nisha couldn't believe they were considering a website redesign (again!). Their site worked on a mobile device, but it was dreadfully slow to load. It was time to build a new site. Having gone through the process a couple of times before, Brent and Nisha wanted to futureproof their website as much as possible. Their web designer said they could stick with WordPress since they were familiar with it, but they needed to prioritize the mobile experience during the site redesign. It's been a few years now since that site (Brent and Nisha's third) went live. It's still working well for them... for now.

———

IN THE NEW world of web, your site has to work on all the things. And, right now, that list of things is growing exponentially. Next time you're at the shopping mall, pop into a computer or mobile phone store. Have a look at all the different devices. Laptop computers, desktop computers, large screen displays, tablets, smartphones... the amount of electronics connected to the internet is mind-boggling.

There are so many different types, all with different screen shapes and sizes. Your website needs to be optimized for all of them. Gulp.

The list of internet-enabled devices isn't limited to electronics with screens either. We've seen a real increase in the amount of voice-enabled technologies in the marketplace. More and more of us are using voice assistants (like Alexa, Google Home, or Siri) to find information on the web and read it aloud for us. Is your website ready for this technology?

Good news: it likely is. As long as you're optimizing your site for search engines (I'll go over that in chapter 7), you're also making your website voice assistant–friendly. The metadata (the data that's invisibly coded into your site to explain to the internet what your information means) is relatively the same for Google search as it is for a Google Home device.

The reason I bring all this up is that, in this fast-moving digital age, you have to think about voice, video, and virtual environments when it comes to conceptualizing your online home. More and more people are using mobile devices to browse and search the internet, and small business owners must ensure their websites are attracting these potential customers. You need to make sure that whatever web solutions you choose set you up for success as we move towards a super-connected world.

Modern websites: Mobile and responsive

People are turning to their mobile devices first for their email, social media, maps, and Google searches, rather than their desktop or laptop computers. Across the internet, the amount of web traffic coming from desktop and laptop computers is declining, and the amount coming from smartphones is rising. In fact, Google is now crawling the mobile version of websites, indexing and ranking the content and structure of the mobile site first, before it looks at what's happening on larger screens.

What this means is that small businesses can no longer afford to think of the mobile web as an afterthought. You need to be where your customers and clients are—and where they're more likely to be in the future. Optimizing your website and digital strategy for mobile and embracing mobile-first thinking now will continue to pay off as mobile search continues to grow.

Responsive design is a digital website format that adapts to each screen, and it's pretty much magic. Okay, it's not magic—responsive design is code. But it feels like magic.

If you have a non-responsive website, or if there's content missing when your site loads on a smartphone, you could be in trouble. Responsive design allows screens of all sizes, including small mobile ones, to view the site properly. Instead of simply shrinking the entire website down at scale, responsive design *responds* to the size of the screen the website is being viewed on, displaying content differently. So, whether someone is seeing your site on a phone-sized screen or at tablet size or on a laptop computer, a responsive website automatically adapts to the screen on which it is viewed. In many cases, for example, this type of design displays a new navigation menu better formatted to touch screens as well as readable text sizes, sometimes switching to a single column of text as necessary. The best part of responsive design is that you don't have to go through the administrative headache of making a separate mobile website; you are creating only *one* website, but the way the content is displayed changes, adapting to the screen it's viewed on.

How do you get responsive design on your site?

There are a number of different ways to get there. Square-space and Shopify are responsive design environments, which means that if you've decided to create your website in either of those platforms, it will always adapt to different devices seamlessly. They've done the work for you. In WordPress, most of the newer themes are also responsive. Just make sure that when you're choosing one, either on your own or with a designer or developer, it's labelled as such. If you're building a bigger site or working with a designer or developer directly to create the site, make sure that you ask them about responsive design.

What if you already have a site, and you've now discovered that it's not responsive?

Let me tell you a little story about my own Camp Tech website.

I've long been telling my students about how it's important to scale your website with your business, and that it's so much easier than ever before to DIY. I'm a professionally trained web designer, so I created the first Camp Tech site myself using WordPress so that it would be easy to update and to manage. WordPress is great, and as I've said earlier, it can connect to other systems through plugins. I set up our workshop registration on Eventbrite and used an Eventbrite-to-WordPress plugin to connect the two sites. That way people could visit the Camp Tech website (WordPress) and order tickets for upcoming events (through the Eventbrite hookup), and we'd get a notification every time someone signed up.

Eventually that system fell apart. Eventbrite still worked, but our business changed: people wanted to sign up for multiple classes at once, and Eventbrite doesn't have a shopping cart. It only offered one registration at a time, and our clients got frustrated with having to enter their credit card details over and over again to register for more than one class. We also couldn't offer store-wide bulk discounts or promotions, like "buy one, get one free." Those functionality shortcomings meant that we had to find a different solution.

Were we going to get something made especially for us? I thought about it, but it was going to cost way too much for what Camp Tech could afford at the time. So, we went with another solution: we switched to a Shopify website. It worked better than Eventbrite, but it still wasn't exactly perfect. We had to get professional advice to jam that square peg into a round hole, but it was a solution that served us well.

For a while.

We're now a few years in to our Shopify website, and the cracks are starting to show. We still love the product, but we're not sure that it's going to work for us in our next phase of business development. And that's okay!

What I'm saying here is that there's a limit to how far a single site can take you. How much do you want to invest, and what's the shelf life of a website? How much can you do to make it wonderful, and when might you need to get some help to get up to the speed at which digital devices are moving today? That's up to you. You need to make it easy for your clients to find you, to get the information they need, and, most of all, you need to make it as easy as possible for them to give you money.

If your site isn't doing these things, then it's likely not keeping up with the needs of the modern digital consumer, and you need to start thinking about changing your strategy. It's always a good idea to periodically look around to see how you can add value to your online home.

Need for speed

Having a website that displays well on every device isn't enough. It has to *perform* well too.

There are many factors that determine a website's mobile performance, but the most important one is how fast it loads. In 2018, Google started to regularly take page performance into account when indexing sites (in addition to all the other things Google looks at when crawling a website). What this means for a small business or organization is that if your website isn't working fast, you could be penalized by appearing lower in search engine results.

For website performance diagnostics, run your website through Google's easy-to-use Mobile-Friendly Test (search .google.com/test/mobile-friendly) and Mobile Speed Test (thinkwithgoogle.com/feature/testmysite). If your results are poor, the solutions are likely technical. You'll need to talk to a web developer about why and see what can be optimized. This shouldn't take long: some fixes are really fast, and if you have just this one goal in mind when you have this conversation, the developer may be able to address any challenges in a matter of a few hours. Then you'll be up and running.

Accessibility: The web for all

Just like a store or office in the real world, your online home needs to be designed well and organized coherently, and it has to be physically accessible. Yes, *physically*. The best websites all share a fundamental premise: that people need ease online. We can get caught up in all of the bells and whistles when it comes to web design and development, but sometimes simpler is better.

Simpler isn't better just because it means you'll get folks through your site more easily: it's also the law.

If you are developing a website, it is always important to consider how different people will be able to access your content, because people with visual, auditory, cognitive, and other types of disabilities can and will be using your site. Governments around the world often require websites and web content to conform with what are called the World Wide Web Consortium's Web Content Accessibility Guidelines (WCAG) 2.0 (which you can read at w3.org/WAI/WCAG21/quickref). This is especially important for government and charitable websites, but it ought to be true (and in some places it is) for all businesses, because, let's face it, the internet is for everyone.

Is your website in line with the WCAG guidelines? You can start by looking at your website through the WAVE Web Accessibility Evaluation Tool (wave.webaim.org). This tool assesses whether or not your site meets the global WCAG standards for accessibility for people with a range of needs.

It isn't always going to be that straightforward, because accessibility isn't solely about making your website work for people with disabilities. Every website visitor wants to be able to scan quickly through a site to find the thing they want to read, and they don't want to be encumbered by a lot of slogging: closing pop-ups, pausing video, and getting lost as they struggle to find their way through small or badly designed navigation menus.

Let's talk about how to think through the accessibility options that you might not have considered, especially if you have a number of different functions on your online home.

- **Make navigation your number-one concern.** More than anything, people need to find their stuff, their options, and what they're looking for. Don't hide the way: make it easy for them. Remember when we talked about using web conventions in the last chapter? Don't fight those. Don't make your menu hard to find or navigate, and keep a site map link at the bottom of the page in case someone gets lost.

- **Your information and design components must be easy to read.** Think about the size and shape of your fonts, and the colour contrasts that you choose for each page: are they small and hard-coded (for example, by your web developer) to stay the same size? Responsive design should enable the site to shift to large print automatically. What if someone looking at your site has colour blindness, which affects up to 8 percent of all men (and 0.5 percent of women) in the world? Never use colour alone to communicate important information (e.g., "click the red button"). Think about decreasing the use of red and green in particular in key information areas on your site, and make sure there's enough contrast between the colours you are featuring. The WebAIM accessibility checker will tell you if your text colour passes or fails the WCAG colour contrast threshold.

- **You need *alt text*.** Many of us can see images on websites, but those with visual impairments can't. It's not fair that they miss out on the imagery of a website. Blind people often use screen reader software that reads the internet to them. When screen readers get to an image, they read what's called the "alt(ernative) text" aloud. Alt text should describe the image, but if you don't put it in, it will just say "image" or the image's file name. It's on you to add the alt text to your website's images, and many web builder tools have a prompt for you to do this. Put in a short, succinct description of the picture (for example, if it's an image of a cute puppy sleeping, put "cute puppy sleeping" as the alt text). Someone hearing the alt text of a website read aloud should receive the same information as someone looking at the picture.

- **Make sure videos aren't distracting.** Auto-playing videos (and audio) are difficult to pause or stop, which can cause confusion or frustration for almost every user. Sure, video is an important part of the new world of web, but it has to be a choice, not an imposition.

- **Same thing goes with animation.** Animation can often be annoying to users, and if it's loud and bright and pops up suddenly, it can even be dangerous to people with specific medical conditions such as epilepsy or heart conditions. Pay attention to what you think would be fun versus what will actually work to advance your strategy: which is your foremost goal?

What do you like on other websites? Do that.

When it comes to responsiveness, speed, and accessibility, you *can* trust your gut instincts.

Because, really, this is all about you. You're a consumer and an information gatherer too. You know what it's like to get lost in a maze of options online and lose sight of what you came to do. You know those things that folks do on their websites that makes you close a tab. It's your job to find a better way. You should aim to create a website that you would like to use, rather than one that's filled with extraneous stuff that, really, only serves to block people from getting what they want out of the experience.

It's also about strategy. Go back to your business goal and test whether you're going to get bang for your buck (time-wise or financial!) if you add one more thing to your site. If your designer or developer or, heck, your best friend says that you need a bit more pizzazz, check in with yourself: is that going to make an impact on my clients or my business, or is it going to create a sideline away from what I want to achieve?

Trust yourself in knowing what kind of experience would be right for your clients or customers. That doesn't mean you can't feel free to be that child in the sandbox, trying out new ways of doing things; in fact, I encourage it. You don't need to feel afraid that you'll get it wrong. This is the internet, after all. You can change things up in the click of a button. Know that change will be constant and roll with it.

. . . .

CHAPTER 4 FROM 30,000 FEET

You need to optimize your website for the growing number of internet-enabled devices in the consumer marketplace.

. . . .

Responsive design means your website adapts to the device it's being viewed on.

. . . .

Page load speed is essential in both Google's eyes and your customers'. If your website is slow, run it through Google's Mobile Speed Test for insight into why.

. . . .

Follow the WCAG 2.0 guidelines for website accessibility, and design your site with accessibility and ease of use in mind. It's not just the right thing to do; in many areas of the world, it's the law.

. . . .

What do you like on other people's websites? Do that. What annoys you on other people's websites? Don't do that.

. . . .

5

Lock It Down: Digital Privacy, Data Security, and the Law

EVERY ONCE IN a while, I receive an email from a past web design client with a subject line like, "HELP! My site has been hacked!"... and then they go downhill from there. One of the worst instances of this was with my client Lauren, a photographer. I helped Lauren get her WordPress website online and taught her how to keep it properly maintained (always updating the WordPress software and plugins, as well as running regular backups and security scans). I hadn't heard from Lauren in years when she emailed me in a panic, saying her site was full of spam content, and when she googled her business name, a warning came up in the search result saying, "The site ahead contains malware." That meant that anyone visiting Lauren's website could get a virus, which is *not* a good look for any business!

Turns out, Lauren wasn't keeping her WordPress website up-to-date, and the site had been hacked. Unfortunately, it happens more often than you might guess. The good news is there's a service called Sucuri (sucuri.net) that cleans websites fairly quickly. I helped Lauren get connected to Sucuri, which cleaned her site and submitted a request to Google to remove the malware warning. Within 24 hours, Lauren's website was healthy again, and she definitely learned her lesson about keeping her WordPress software up-to-date.

IF YOU WENT to a restaurant and there was a public health warning on the door, would you ever go back? Customer and client trust is a very important part of your brand. It is for every company. Trust has to be built before people buy your products or try your services, and this is built through the online experience as much as it is through the in-person one.

In order to gain and keep trust, you need to ensure that your site is secure in order to protect people's identities and assets. We know that cybersecurity risks are highest when there is a lack of care given to data management and protection, because this allows hackers to access and leach your customers' and clients' personal information, money, and password access and therefore put them at risk. To this end, we need to control data and information on our websites in order to create barriers to prevent breaches.

For most companies, this is where information technology (IT) comes in. People who specialize in IT don't simply install software and keep computers running. They're also the good hackers of the world: they block what other people try to steal, and they do it, in many cases, using the same tools and resources that the bad guys use.

Of course, many small businesses don't have a dedicated IT department. But there are things that could go wrong, and it's important to have your security properly configured, to protect yourself, your information, and everything that your clients have inputted into your website.

In this chapter, we'll get into the essential tools you need for digital safety and security.

A PICNIC (problem in chair, not in computer) problem

Here's something you may not know: *people* are the biggest risk to digital security, not the technology itself. And I don't mean hackers; I mean you and your team. Digital security should be practiced daily; it should become a habit just as much as your physical safety is.

To see why this is the case, let's take a quick look at the three biggest concerns in digital security today: *phishing*, *data breaches*, and *malware*.

Phishing is the most prevalent of cybercrimes. These are spam emails that look like they're coming from people or a company you know, such as a bank you use. Also increasing in frequency are text messages and direct messages (DMs) on social media with the same aim in mind. If you follow the links provided, you're led to counterfeit websites designed to trick you into divulging your financial data, or your computer may get infected with a virus that does the same thing, except without your knowledge. Most modern email systems like Gmail pick these up and discard them, because the email server that sent them doesn't match the visible email address, but some can slip through the cracks.

The type of **data breaches** that are employed by hackers are shifting every year, but they're mostly about password protection. With so many digital accounts, it is (unfortunately) highly possible that platforms will have a data breach. That's why password management—and having a different password for different logins—is very important. If, for some reason, your password gets shared in a data breach, and you only have one password, someone could easily access several of your accounts with that password.

Malware is an umbrella term for all kinds of nasty stuff that can impact your systems if you're not careful. It includes viruses, Trojans, worms, spyware, and perhaps the scariest of all—ransomware. Ransomware is a type of computer virus that locks you out of all your files until you pay a fee (ransom) to a hacker to unlock it for you. A lot of malware comes from phishing attempts (see above), but it can also come from clicking on iffy ads online.

How to protect yourself

Okay, let's start with you and your office. We'll get to protecting your clients in a moment, but let's get your house in order first.

1 **Use a password manager.** In an ideal world, all online passwords would be insanely long and complicated *and* different for each login. On the whole, however, it is better to have a *different* password for everything than a *complicated* password. If you have the same password

everywhere, no matter how complex it is, if it's compromised in one place, then it's compromised everywhere (see sidebar for an ironic story about this). The problem with having a different password for every login is the headache of having to remember all those different passwords!

You may have a little book where you write down all your passwords, which is fine... except what happens if you forget the book? Or you could have all your passwords stored in a document on your computer or in the Notes section of your phone... but that's not encrypted and if someone can access that file, they have access to everything.

I recommend using a password manager, which is a type of software or app that keeps track of your passwords for you. It's like a secure version of the little book or the passwords document, but a password manager is password protected itself. Here's how it works: with a password manager, you have a unique and strong password for every secure website, but you never have to remember any of them, except for your master password, which unlocks the whole system. A password manager automatically logs you in to wherever you need to be on the web, and you'll never have to type your passwords again; you can make them as long and as complex as you want. You'll need to do some work and, in some cases, pay a few dollars a month for a good password manager, but if you choose the right secure system, like LastPass or 1Password, you only have to update your master password. Do that about once a month, and you're golden.

DO AS I SAY, NOT AS I DO

MY ADVICE FOR you about passwords is nothing you haven't heard before. Having a different, complex password for every digital account (and updating it regularly) is something that we all know we should do. But many, including the biggest names in technology, don't follow their own advice. In 2016, a very large data breach at LinkedIn saw the passwords of millions of accounts leaked online. One of the accounts that had its password leaked belonged to Facebook CEO Mark Zuckerberg. His password was quickly discovered (and exploited) by hackers, who revealed that the tech titan was breaking two of the cardinal rules of password security. Zuckerberg wasn't using a complex password (it was "dadada") and he was using the same password in multiple places. According to a *Vanity Fair* article, the simple phrase that logged him in to his LinkedIn account also granted access to his Pinterest and Twitter accounts. Talk about someone who should know better.

2   **Keep everything updated.** You know that little prompt that you get on your laptop or smartphone to update your operating system, apps, or software? DO THAT.

More often than not, these updates are security patches. I know, they always pop up at the most inopportune time, say, when you have a presentation in 10 minutes or have to run to a doctor's appointment. I give you permission to press the ignore button once! But

that's it. You have to keep on top of software updates.
For computers, Macs tend to be a little more secure
than PCs, but they are still susceptible to viruses and
other challenges. Owners of any and all digital devices
need to configure them correctly. This isn't limited to
computers—there are safety and security vulnerabilities in smartphones too (Android phones more so than
iPhones, although no device has perfect security).

3 **Don't blindly trust anti-virus tools.** Anti-virus software
can detect threats, and it can also give you a false sense
of security. If you're going to run anti-virus software,
don't rely on it alone. Instead, you need to practice digital security on a routine basis. This includes blocking
advertisements from your web browser using an instantly
downloadable plugin for your browser, such as GetAd
Block.com.

4 **Protect your wifi activity: use a VPN.** A virtual private
network (VPN) is a type of software that makes sure that
whatever you're doing online is encrypted. Whenever
you're on a non-password-protected internet source like
an open wifi network at a coffee shop or airport, you definitely need to boot up a VPN program. It should work
on any number of devices—you can have VPN software
on your computer and also on your mobile devices. One
of my regular go-to websites is Wirecutter: it has independent reviews of consumer tech products, and they
maintain a great list of VPN recommendations (thewire
cutter.com/reviews/best-vpn-service).

5 **Whenever possible, pass the responsibility up the food
chain.** Use the power of tools made for protecting data.

If you can get it off your own desk, do it. For example, if you use a plain spreadsheet on your laptop to house your client data versus an encrypted customer database that keeps its information safely secured in the cloud, then you're setting your system up for failure. If you are ever subjected to phishing, everything on your computer could be up for grabs. Lean harder on bigger tools. Although online or cloud-based systems often have a fee, they're worth it. You don't have time (or expertise) to deal with a breach or a scam. For example, some messaging apps on smartphones aren't totally secure. The most secure messaging app I recommend is Signal (signal.org), which offers end-to-end encryption.

6 **Practice digital hygiene in the office.** Remind everyone: email is about as secure as sending a postcard in the mail. Be very careful about the amount and type of information you are sending in or attaching to an email. And for the love of DOS, don't ever send credit card information in an email!

A big part of keeping the whole office secure is ensuring that everyone has their own logins to digital systems and deciding who has access to what ahead of time. Don't have a shared login for any system or software. Take three minutes and create new accounts for each user. If you do this, then when someone leaves the company, or when a breach happens, you'll be able to manage your systems properly. There are such things as user permission levels, especially in website content management systems such as WordPress and in social media professional pages such as Facebook—each individual can access a different level of functionality. This means that your marketing intern could be given access to your email newsletter open rate in Mailchimp but not your billing information.

7   **Use two-factor authentication.** If a program offers you two-factor authentication (or the similar, but slightly different, two-step authentication), use it! This system means you log in with your password and provide a second verification on another device before it logs you in.

8   **Having a plan is better than nothing.** Stress test everything you're doing to protect your data! I used to wake up in the middle of the night worried about what would happen if a teammate left her laptop in a taxi: could we wipe the files from a distance so that personal information would not be stolen or get her files off it so that we wouldn't lose our work? Don't wait until the worst happens. Do a fire drill and work out all of the details of your digital security plan with everyone on your team before disaster strikes.

Your customers, your responsibilities

Not only do you have to protect your office, but there are a number of legal potholes you'll want to avoid out there in cyberspace so that you can do right by your customers and clients.

Some of this is already built into the software you used to create your website, and some is automatically embedded into additions to your web presence, such as online store systems and social media. Most software out there uses encryption to hide data in the right way and to prevent unauthorized use.

But that's not always the case. You may find yourself on the wrong side of the law if you're not taking security seriously.

It doesn't have to be a big slog, even though there's a lot on your shoulders. In fact, the legal requirements for web security are, I think, making things a bit less difficult over time. That's because we're all being held to a higher standard: our sites have to start with safety and security, which means that most of the digital tools that you're likely going to be using have already gone through their own checks and balances.

It's your job, nonetheless, to be the last line of defence. You're the last checkpoint. And you *can* keep your customers safe.

Let's take a look at everything you need for you and your customers to feel safe and to be safe online.

Your customers' data is your responsibility

Legally and ethically, there are concrete steps for companies to follow to make sure that customers' privacy and data are protected.

But let's back up: in law, three parties are responsible for the protection of data.

1   **Consumers themselves.** People have rights to protect their own privacy either by not being active participants online or by limiting the way in which they choose to interact with websites, such as by refusing to accept cookies or shutting down push notification options.

2   **Internet service providers (ISPs).** These businesses map all data transactions and share and sell aggregate data with third parties as a matter of course, but they are also expected to put up firewalls to make sure that this doesn't happen without client permission.

3   **Online software creators,** including the companies that
create website platforms, which develop and sell the
means to package data. All businesses that have websites,
for example, are able to choose what, how, and when they
collect data from users and customers, and what they will
do with this data either internally or externally. If you
use online software in your business, you're a part of this
group. This suggests that it is software developers that
are the most responsible for whether or not someone's
data is private, as they control data input and use, but
this is not entirely true. Software makers have privacy
responsibilities but so do you. That means that you, as a
business or organization, have a responsibility to manage
this process carefully.

That having been said, there are different guidelines
based on how you come into contact with your customer
data.

What exactly is the law?

Basic legal standards include Canada's Anti-Spam Legislation (CASL) and the Personal Information Protection
and Electronic Documents Act (PIPEDA) in Canada, and
the General Data Protection Regulation (GDPR) laws in
the European Union (plus the United Kingdom, Norway,
Lichtenstein, and Iceland). In the United States, the situation is a little more abstract. California has best-practice
level privacy standards, but outside California, it differs from
state to state. The American Civil Liberties Union suggests
that companies comply with the GDPR globally by 2020,
as this is expected to be the international standard.

Here's how I see it, though. You might as well be compli-
ant to the strictest laws out there as soon as you can. Why?

Even if someone's only interaction with you online is reading your newsletter, if they are in the European Union, Iceland, Norway, Lichtenstein, or the United Kingdom, then the GDPR applies to your connection with them.

The GDPR is a huge piece of legislation with many layers. The part that most directly impacts small business is around consent: people have to be given the right to explicitly opt in to marketing communication and opt in to being tracked online. For example, you can't just buy email addresses or collect them willy-nilly. You have to ask people's permission to send them information either through email or through your website or social media, and you can't then sell their information to others without users specifically saying that's okay.

So, how *do* you make sure your clients are safe?

First and foremost, know that **if it feels wrong, it's probably wrong.** If you don't feel comfortable doing something and would be ashamed to look a client in the face if they knew what you were doing, then you shouldn't be doing it. Don't keep data in an easily accessible place in the office where anyone could see it, don't purchase email addresses, and don't try to scam the system in social media by buying likes from digital farms. None of these practices will serve your business or organizational interests over the long run.

Know where your client data is. Make a list of all the places online where you are collecting personally identifiable information (PII). Start with your website. Are you requesting names, email addresses, or credit card information? Online forms, comment boxes, email marketing signups, and ecommerce are all places where you may be collecting personal data. Looking beyond your website, where else are you collecting, storing, and using customer or client data? Think about sales databases, customer relationship management software, and email marketing lists.

Check your exposure. You need to have a clear under-standing of where all of the data is housed. Is this data kept on your own website server? On your computers' hard drives? Or inside third-party software? If you have data on your own server, you may be exposed to risk.

Understand why you're collecting data. The law wants to make sure that you have a good reason to collect personal information in the first place. If someone wants to buy some-thing from you, that's a good enough reason. But you still need explicit permission from your clients and a clear record of that consent being given. In other words, when they share their data, your clients should also be filling in a form stat-ing that it's okay for you to collect and keep that data. What doesn't count as consent are things like pre-ticked opt-in boxes: your clients have to choose *actively* to give consent. If they simply don't say no to being included in your data-base, both PIPEDA and GDPR consider that unlawful. Same goes if a client hasn't been active on your site or system for a while: you need to trigger a new consent form for them to sign off on.

Find out how your website tracks visitors. Cookies, web beacons, and "tracking pixels" are tracking tools that allow web browsers to remember information about the web-site visitor's browsing session. They track things like what device your clients are using, where they're located, which pages of the website they visited, and more. Some of that information can be personally identifiable, so you may have a legal responsibility to manage that information with care. Under the GDPR, for example, it is not enough to have pas-sive consent for the use of cookies (through a message such as, "If you continue to use this website, you agree to our terms"). Instead, website visitors must indicate their aware-ness and agreement *before* cookies, web beacons, and pixels load and start tracking. You can use a tool like Iubenda (iubenda.com/en) to help you do this correctly.

Use third-party data processors when possible. If you collect PII, you're the *data collector*. But you can also rely on other services to process the data. They're the *data processor*. Companies like Google, Mailchimp, Facebook, PayPal, Stripe (or any other payment gateway) are data processors, and if you use their services, you need to have an agreement with them. This agreement is called a data processing agreement (DPA) and it ensures that both you (the data collector) and the third party (the data processor) are handling data with appropriate care and responsibility. Having signed DPAs with third-party data processors acknowledges that you've done your due diligence and are only processing data with those that take the law seriously. It doesn't mean that you'll never be under scrutiny, though: make sure you check the reliability and security of the companies from whom you are buying software or whose systems you use on a regular basis.

Create a privacy policy and plan to use it every day

With all of these new laws coming into play, it's necessary to have a privacy policy for your customers and clients.

Once you've collected all of your data points and checked out your vulnerabilities, you're going to want to come up with an outward-facing privacy policy and an inward-facing privacy plan. Here are a few steps to get that underway.

First, create a privacy policy: the set of rules that determines how you'll use data. This is a legal document to which your clients can refer if and when they need to. Your privacy policy must be concise, easy to understand, and clear, and it should include the following information:

- What information are you collecting?
- Exactly how are you collecting it?
- Why is it necessary for you to collect it?
- What are you doing to keep the information safe?
- Is the data ever shared with third parties?
- How can someone can get in touch with you to access their data or request its removal?

You can use a privacy policy generator like FreePrivacy Policy.com or TermsFeed.com/Privacy-Policy-Generator to make a simple document for you and then add to it as needed.

Publish your privacy policy where it can be seen by anyone (I recommend putting a link to it in the footer of your website). If anything changes, you need to update your privacy policy and inform your clients and customers when it's updated.

Next, create an internal privacy plan. This is how you will manage privacy in your work environment, and how you'll help your team to be responsible for your clients' security and privacy.

1   Display your privacy policy in a prominent place, both online and in your office. Publish a Privacy Policy page on your website.

2   Understand what personally identifiable information you (and your website) are collecting and keep a file on how you are managing that data.

3   Have a plan laid out for how you'll protect that information: add your third-party vendors that are under DPAs to that list, as well as places where you are personally responsible for data.

4 If a customer asks about what personally identifiable information you have about them, you should be prepared to share it and be able to delete it completely.

5 Train your team on how to keep private data secure and the privacy practices of your business.

6 Under the rules of the GDPR, if you suffer a data breach, you have to report it to the impacted individuals and the necessary authorities within 72 hours.

This is the big stuff, friends: taking care of the people who butter your bread. It's important not just because it's the law, but because repeat business is the best kind of business. Whether you're selling purses, connecting with community members, or planning the biggest product launch of your career, you need to make sure that your clients are right there with you, and that your work doesn't get sidelined with the kind of technical breach that can kneecap your reputation in an instant.

. . . .

CHAPTER 5 FROM 30,000 FEET

Even if you don't have an on-site IT department, keeping your customer and client data secure is very important.
. . . .

You can prevent three of the biggest threats to data privacy (phishing, data breaches, and malware):

→ Use a password manager.
→ Update your systems regularly.

→ Don't blindly trust anti-virus tools.
→ Use a VPN.
→ Practice digital hygiene in the office.
→ Use two-factor authentication.

. . . .

Your customers' data is your responsibility, and depending on where you do business, you could be subject to data laws including the General Data Protection Regulation (GDPR). To comply, you should regularly:

→ review your company's data collection practices; and
→ create a privacy policy and a privacy plan, and share it with your team and your customers.

. . . .

6

Content Is King

DEBRA HAD ENOUGH of the rat race. After years of commuting from outside the city to the downtown core every day to work in a large law firm, Debra said enough was enough and decided to set up her own boutique legal practice in her community. She knew that she needed a website, so she built her own site using Squarespace with a simple template. She wrote the messaging on the site herself, listing what kind of law she practiced (family law), what services she offered, and how people could get in touch. The problem was the copy on Debra's website was really dry. It used too much legal jargon and didn't make sense to Debra's ideal client—real people who needed help with real-life situations.

Debra's office assistant had a background in marketing and gently encouraged Debra to reconsider the content of her website. Instead of being so stiff, the messaging on the site needed to tell the story of Debra's career and how she helped her clients. It needed to focus on the solutions Debra could provide and convey the sense of warmth and empathy that clients feel when they work with her.

Fortunately, Debra was a good listener. She worked with her office assistant to find the sweet spot with the website, rewriting the content to both reflect what she did and attract the right kind of client for her boutique law office. It told her story—and kept it from having an unhappy ending.

EVERYONE WANTS TO hear a story. No matter what business you're in, and no matter where you live in the world, you're going to be asked: What's your story? Why did you decide to do what you do? What makes you different from everyone else out there?

You need to be ready to tell your story on your website, on social media platforms, as well as in every customer inter-action. The funny thing is that even though our business stories are very personal, not everyone knows what it means to tell that story well or how to create content to reach the audience they need to build a business.

In this chapter, we're going to explore how to write killer web content. We're going to create that content with your ideal customer or client in mind, while also thinking about search engines like Google, so the right people can find you when they're searching.

Throw away the elevator pitch

One of the most important (and difficult!) things about developing content to market your business is deciding what you want to say. Finding your voice, using your own vocabulary, and engaging with the way your industry talks about your products or services is key.

Business gurus would say that part of the process of deciding what story you want to tell is creating what they call an elevator pitch. This one perfectly crafted sentence is how you'd describe your business idea if you happened to meet investment icon Warren Buffett on the elevator. Warren has a lot of money, and he's invested in more businesses than maybe any individual on the planet. You'd have about 30 seconds to make an impact before the doors fly open, and Warren is gone forever. Warren, they say, is the ultimate arbiter of whether or not a business will be successful, so it makes sense that you'd want to impress him.

But do you?

I'm going to hazard a guess that Warren Buffett isn't your target customer. He's probably not actually interested in buying your products and services any more than a random stranger on the street. And here's the thing: your story doesn't have to appeal to just anyone—or to everyone. It has to appeal to one single group: the people who are already interested in what you do, namely your target clients and customers.

Instead of trying to explain your business to Warren Buffet in a single sentence, imagine describing it to a past client or customer that you haven't seen in a while. How would you talk about your ideas in a way they would understand? How would you tell your story to someone who is already interested in what you have to say but wants to know more? Think about what it's like to share something that you value with someone who wants to listen: that's what it's like talking to your customers.

And here's another secret that no one ever tells you.

People want to talk about themselves. They want their own story to be heard. This means that your content is not about you. It's about how people see themselves reflected in your brand and the experiences that they can have with that brand. The stories that you tell on your website and in your social media therefore have to resonate with your clients' own life experiences, values, and wishes for themselves.

The great thing is that you have a lot in common with your potential clients: you're both interested in your products and services. People don't seek out a new pair of shoes or a new massage therapist if they don't already want to do so. This means that you likely share a common point of view, need, or aesthetic style. The trick is finding where that commonality lies.

EXERCISE: CHILL AND SPILL

START PAYING ATTENTION to what you love to read, look at, and explore on the internet. One afternoon, grab a cold beer or your favourite coffee, and take some time to pay attention to what you want to read online. Just let yourself travel the web in any direction. Write down what you like and don't like about what you read. What speaks to you? What site made you stay the longest? Why? Was it beautiful photographs, a thoughtful essay, the ease of reading, or a focus on video over text?

Often the answer to these questions will surprise you, but it's worth creating your own opinion about content before you start developing words for your own website.

Don't forget about the robots

Diana, a client of mine who had moved to Canada from her native Denmark, sells the most beautiful luxury furniture from her home country. Everything in her store is exquisitely designed and crafted, and the website that I designed for her, if I do say so myself, was gorgeous. Diana decided to write the content for her site, based on her own standards of the best possible brand message.

One day, Diana emailed me. She said that she was googling "luxury Scandinavian furniture," and her site didn't come up. Not on the first page of Google and not on any subsequent pages. I had to tell her something shocking: she didn't actually use the words "luxury Scandinavian furniture" anywhere on her site. She was so deeply engaged in her own point of view that she hadn't included the obvious keywords. Diana has since overhauled the content of her website accordingly, and she now ranks for the keywords she wants in Google searches.

WHEN YOU WRITE your content yourself, you sometimes forget the obvious. Unless you are in a technical field where a customer will naturally understand your industry jargon, you also have to keep it simple. There's another important lesson here: Diana was so focused on targeting her website content to her customers, she forgot about the search robots.

In order to get listed properly on Google and other search engines, you need to add the right content and keywords to your site on a regular basis. This increases your *search engine optimization (SEO)*, so that more people will find your site through web searches. Largely mechanical, SEO means that you have to sprinkle proper keywords and phrases throughout the site, in order to ensure search engines index your content accurately.

When your website rises in search engine results, it drives more traffic to your site. This is the ultimate goal of SEO. But it's not just any web traffic you want—it's the *right* web traffic. SEO isn't about trying to trick Google into indexing and ranking your website highly; it's about indexing your site *properly*.

The best way to approach SEO is by evolving your site into something that holds actual value to your clients over the long term. The difficulty is that most people aren't prepared to do the work that organic search optimization (read: not a Google Ad) requires, which is getting to know your customers and your industry on a deep level. Your clients' needs—and what words they actually use to communicate their needs in search engine queries—have to come first.

We'll talk about how to get the most out of the technology during your SEO planning in the next chapter. But right now, we need to start with the foundation, which is creating the quality content that you need to impress your people.

You do you

The reality is that we're in a new world of the web where content is king. It drives search, it builds community, and it has a direct impact on your bottom line. Even though you have to ensure that your site doesn't ignore the search engine bots, you have to appeal to humans first and robots second.

When it comes to creating great content, start with being yourself. What you can do to make your content better is to share what is important to you. Everyone around you is experiencing tech fatigue and communication burnout, and we're overwhelmed by the amount of content that we consume on a daily basis. That's why you need to have, and share, your actual opinions. Of course you have something to say! What's your jam? Puppies? Norwegian history? Shoes? The internet is not a place where you have to be afraid of having a personality. In fact, the internet is a place where people respond to emotion and opinions. Think of the kind of content that gets shared online. Stories of adversity and triumph spread like wildfire. So do stories that are funny or enraging. I encourage you to be bold with your writing online. Don't hedge. Take a stand on a subject, have an opinion, and put it out there.

Images

The best thing you can do to make your website extraordinary is to use your own images (as long as they're decent quality—skip the blurry, poorly lit photos). People are much more likely to respond to your call to action if they like what they see. Don't be afraid of hiring a photographer for a few hours; often they're cheaper than you might expect, and you'll get images (for which you have copyright) that highlight the best aspects of your products, services, and brand identity.

If you want to find images online, don't rely on a Google image search, Pinterest, or Instagram: you will likely be in breach of someone else's copyright. Instead, conduct a Creative Commons search (search.creativecommons.org) for photographs that can be used for commercial purposes, or subscribe to a royalty-free, stock photography service like Shutterstock or 500px to get images at a fraction of full prices.

Note: "royalty-free" doesn't mean you-don't-have-to-pay free. It just means you don't have to pay extra royalties to the artist to use the image in a variety of settings. Be prepared to search for several minutes (or even hours) to get the exact image you want. Keep in mind, however, that if you use an image from a royalty-free stock service, or even a totally free image site like Unsplash (unsplash.com), you run the risk of seeing that image everywhere. Your brand could be confused with another if you use a very popular image for your homepage or logo, so you may want to use stock photographs for secondary pages or posts, rather than for your primary imagery.

Words

The crux of developing your content is copywriting.

Everyone can write, but it can be hard to write in a way that makes the right impact. Just like hiring a photographer to enhance your website visitor's experience, it can make business sense to get your website copy written professionally, at least in the beginning. You can find your voice more easily by collaborating with someone who can help you shape your words, either through writing or editing your ideas. You want your website's content to align with your business strategy, and paying for examples that show you the right direction forward may be worth your while.

If the thought of writing your own web copy makes you cringe and you'd rather do anything but, then you might want to get some assistance from a professional writer. If you're searching for a professional copywriter, one of my favourite places to look is on other small business websites that have great copy. Be sure it's not a business you directly compete with. Reach out to the company (a cold email or a phone call to their office usually works) and compliment them on their website. Explain that you're a small business owner (again, not a competitor) and you're looking for a copywriter. Ask if they hired someone, and if so, could they provide a referral?

Once you do track down a potential copywriter, be sure to ask for samples of their work, and ask them about their process. Also, get references from past clients (and actually contact them).

If you're willing to take on the process yourself, there are some key things that you can do to make your writing work for your business.

1 **Keep it short.** How many times have you looked at a screen full of solid text and felt your eyes glaze over and your brain start to fog? Or realized that while you thought you were reading, you've really been skipping down every couple of paragraphs and you're not quite sure if you got the point of the article? Research by CoSchedule and

Buffer says that articles should be 1,200 to 1,500 words to ensure that they meet search engine standards, but research by Nielsen says that the average person will not read more than 300 words before giving up. It's hard to find that sweet spot, but TL;DR (too long; didn't read) is a reality, and if you're not sure what your users want to read, make sure you get to your point quickly.

2   **Make it catchy.** Don't create content for the sake of filling the space. Everything you put on the page needs to be there for a reason (see #1). Think about what matters to people right at that moment: What commonly trends during this time of year? What are some current events happening now? You can use Google or Twitter trending topics to find out what people want to read about.

3   **Make it flow.** People love lists. You're reading one right now for that very reason! Tell people you've got five great ideas to share about saving money on their next vacation, and you'll get their attention. Use numbers! Creating a list helps people to skim through text and find what they're looking for quickly, and they'll love you for it.

4   **Create headings and subheadings.** Google and other search tools prioritize content that has a lot of structure to it, and readers love to skim text online. Break up your text with a lot of headings to keep things clear for your readers. If you want to improve your chances of creating a great heading, you can always use a free tool like CoSchedule.com/Headline-Analyzer to find the word combination that lands better with an online audience.

5 **Use pictures and infographics.** We'll talk about different types of content in the next part of this chapter, but even within written texts, consider including illustrations to make your point.

6 **Tailor to your market segments.** What are the topics your audience is interested in, and what would be helpful to them? If you understand your audience well, you can create content that works. Try scanning comments from your previous posts or from your social media to find out what matters to your customers. Does the topic provide an opportunity for open discussions from your audience? Does your content ask for opinions, so that, next time, you can cater to your customers' needs more easily?

You want your website content to be of high quality for two reasons. The first is always for your target customer or client: you want to appeal to them and engage them with your products or services. The second reason you want your website to have killer web content is for inbound links. In essence, you want other websites to link to your own because this will make marketing easier: you'll get a higher search rank and you'll have people directing potential clients to your site. We'll talk more about inbound links in the next chapter.

It pays to add a bit of content to your site every week because Google likes freshly updated websites. It gives a signal to Google, telling it you're active. Many SEO professionals will tell you that the best way to add content to your site is to have a blog, but this is where I get into friendly arguments with my SEO pals. I agree that fresh content is an important signal for Google, but I have other options for you that don't involve writing all the time.

EXERCISE: THE PROFESSIONAL RANT

START WITH WHAT you love and what you hate, because that's what people will respond to. In your industry, what's a product or service that has amazed you in recent months? Is there some aspect of your business that's alerted you to caution your customers? Was a new regulation announced that will have major repercussions on your industry? Put yourself in your clients' shoes. Create some bullet points on what opportunities and challenges you've noticed, and what advice you'd give your best friends about it. What can you do with your opinions? Do you feel like recording a podcast or writing an opinion piece? How can you communicate your ideas?

A blog is not the only form of content

I'm going to take a load off of your mind: *you are not required to have a blog.*

Sometimes people assume that content has to equal words, but that's not the case anymore. In fact, YouTube is the second largest search engine in the world after Google. You know why. The last time you got stuck putting together that egg-pooping dragon over the holidays when your three-year-old was crying because the egg wasn't opening fast enough, where did you go first? That's right, the Internet Video Education Pitstop. YouTube is filled with some of the most helpful, insightful, and weird content in the world, and you can be a part of it.

Although blogging is a popular way to add content to your site and create that important fresh content for Google, it can quickly become a chore. Writing is one of the most time-intensive tasks in the world (and this is true even for professionals). The internet, social media, and blogging have been around for a while now, and you're not going to amaze your community by making them have to read something new every day. So, unless you absolutely love blogging, keep the writing for specific instructions, technical information, and FAQs on your site, and explore other ways of communicating your brand. There are a range of content development options open to you beyond blogging that will help you achieve your business goals. Let's explore some them.

Video is one of the easiest and most successful strategies for creating content that works. You can record videos right on your laptop or smartphone with your built-in camera and microphone (or invest in some inexpensive equipment if you want extra features). Want to demonstrate how to use your products? Share some advice for frequently asked questions? Become a thought leader in your field? Create short videos and upload them to your website or share them on YouTube, Facebook, Twitter, Instagram, or LinkedIn.

Go live. Consider making a live video on social media where you can interact with your followers in real time. Live streaming video options exist within social media platforms like Facebook, Instagram, Twitter, and YouTube. To "go live," you turn on the live video section inside each platform (if you don't know where it is, look it up on Google), and you're broadcasting in the moment to whoever wants to tune in. Viewers can interact with you by asking questions and commenting on what you're saying, which can be spontaneous and a lot of fun. Going live is great for events as well. Think about recording yourself attending a fashion show, leading a morning meditation, or exploring a new city for your followers to experience right along with you.

Podcasting may be more your style. It can provide you with all of the reach of video, but without the pesky challenge of having to do your hair for the camera on the regular. This is a great option for people who have the gift of the gab and can riff on topics important to an industry, such as financial planning, international development, or city politics. While podcasting is certainly more involved than writing, it can be a great way to demonstrate your expertise and build a community of followers.

Be a guest. Appearing as a guest on other people's podcasts, videos, or blogs is another way to get in front of a new audience. As long as it includes a link back to your site and is shareable, this approach achieves the same results as creating your own content. Reach out and find a bigger community by introducing yourself to other business leaders who have the same audience and offer to host them as well.

Make it work

No matter what approach you use and what platforms you decide are right for your community, content creation is all about great storytelling and authenticity. If you can do you, you'll find hundreds, if not thousands, of people out there that think the way that you do. Find, build, support, and care for your online community, and share your story with them. Share what you really believe about your world, your business, and your future plans. Ask them to share in return and build truly community-driven connections with the people who are on your *side*, not just on your *site*.

. . . .

CHAPTER 6 FROM 30,000 FEET

The most successful website content is honest and authentic and resonates with your target customer or client.

. . . .

Don't steal photos! Use your own, hire a photographer, buy royalty-free photos, or get permission to use other people's.

. . . .

Write your content so it appeals to your human website visitors, but also remember that Google and other search engines are looking at your copy as well.

. . . .

Keep your website content fresh and it will be fresh in the minds of your clients and customers—and stay on top in search engines. Content possibilities include:

→ a blog,
→ a video series,
→ live video,
→ a podcast, and
→ guest appearances on others' podcasts, videos, or blogs.

. . . .

7

SEO

ON APRIL 24, 2012, a penguin crashed the internet. Not a real penguin, a virtual one. Google makes regular updates to its algorithm (the way its search engine works—we'll get into that more in the next pages), and whenever they make a big update, they give it a codename. The algorithm change that started in April 2012 was code-named Penguin, and it had a large impact on a lot of websites.

One of the websites that Penguin affected belonged to Jason, who owns a small but mighty household waste removal business. Jason received a fair bit of website traffic from Google searches—people who were looking to have their junk picked up and disposed of responsibly. He figured he could get even more customers if he appeared on the first page of Google, so he hired someone who said they could help him achieve just that.

Unfortunately, Jason hired the wrong kind of help. The person giving him a hand was gaming the system. They employed a number of shady tactics like keyword stuffing (filling Jason's webpages with words that people could be searching for, over and over again) and link schemes (paying people to link to Jason's website, so it would appear to be more popular in Google's eyes). All of this was to manipulate Jason's site's appearance in Google search results.

For a while, it worked. Jason's website traffic coming from Google was high, and business was doing well. But when Penguin hit, Jason was iced. His website traffic fell by 34 percent in one day and kept falling. Jason fired the "professional" who was helping him and rebuilt his business's reputation slowly over the next few years. Jason is finally seeing the kind of web traffic from Google that he had before the Penguin crash, but this time, he's doing it the right way and earning that traffic organically.

I THINK OF search engine optimization (SEO) as the weight-loss industry of the digital world. It's a multibillion-dollar behemoth determined to find a quick solution for a challenging problem.

It's not a secret to know that, in general, you have to eat less and exercise more to lose weight. It takes time and commitment. The weight-loss industry has been created to find hacks around this challenge: it tells you that it's possible to lose weight faster, if only you follow "simple" tricks. But if you go on a crash diet, you're likely to burn out. SEO is the same. There's a clear formula for SEO, and given time and commitment, anyone can make it work for them. Try to skip the fundamentals, and you'll burn out just like you would on that fad diet.

Let's begin by defining SEO clearly. Search engine optimization (SEO), like I mentioned in the last chapter, enables search engines like Google to connect customers and clients to your site. This is not something that you pay for; it's something that's supposed to happen organically. In general, the more highly ranked a site is on a Google search results page, for example, and more frequently a site appears in the search results list, the more visits it will receive from the search engine's users. That's a good thing.

But it also means that people try hard to get to the top.

What complicates things is that driving more traffic to your website through Google and other search engines is trickier than ever with constant changes in algorithms and rules.

The billion-dollar secret: How does Google work?

Hundreds of factors go into Google's search algorithm; we only know a handful of them at any given time. And they change more often than you would think: as Google and its robots understand what we value and what we want to see, they change the calculation to suit our needs. Why? Well, it's pretty straightforward. In the past, search was all about metadata: what words you actually coded into your site and how well those words matched what people wanted to see. Through your site's metadata, you'd tell Google what you were all about so it could index your site based on what you said. Now, Google can scan all of the stuff on your site itself—not only the words on the pages and the metadata but also photos, videos, and even the layout of the site. Google no longer relies on you to tell it about your website; the search bots can figure it out on their own.

What matters to them? More than you think. Let's go over a few of the search algorithm factors we know Google takes into consideration.

- The website itself. Google notes things like:

  → your website's speed;
  → whether you have a responsive site or one that is optimized for mobile;
  → whether or not you have clean, well-written code;
  → whether or not the website is secure;
  → how much web traffic the website gets;
  → how many links to the website there are in the world, and how popular and trustworthy those linking websites are; and
  → all of the content on the website.

- The person doing the search. Google also factors in who is looking for information, including their:

  → location,
  → past search history, and
  → internet behaviour.

All of these factors are going to be examined in an instant by Google. We're talking finger-snap fast. What actually lands on the search engine results page (SERP) is going to depend on how you meet all of those criteria, all at once, and how best you match what the person is searching for. Extensive cross-cultural and cross-industry research has told Google that people look for very specific things when they visit a website before they deem it credible. If your site is lacking these elements, search engines will continue to scan through other sites until they find what they need.

Black hats aren't going to help

Black-hat SEO solutions offer you hacks to break through the crowd on search engines, but just like losing those final 10 (or 20) pounds, it's going to take time to achieve your goals for good. Search engine marketing (SEM), also known as paid ads, aren't going to make or break your site's ranking either.

What do I mean by "black hat"? Think about it this way: there's an old-timey cowboy in the corner of the room who is always willing to pull out his gun to solve a problem, rather than do the work to talk out his differences over a cup of tea. In the web world, there are some methods that seem like a magic bullet, but really, they're more like magic beans. In the case of SEO, for example, a black-hat approach is one in which you pay for tricks that bump up your visitors and search ranking. The challenge with these tricks is that they're often a short-term solution; they're both superficial and artificial. When you pay click farms—shady services that artificially boost clicks on your website—that's not *real* web traffic. Sure, it can send a short-term signal to Google that your site must be popular, but it won't last. The algorithms used by search engines change rapidly over time. That means that all of your technical work goes down the drain as fast as the folks at Google can code. It's not worth your time to pay for tricks: put on a white hat and invest in yourself and your community by building towards quality, not quantity.

The three components of SEO

The three components of a winning SEO strategy for small business are on-page SEO, off-page SEO, and local SEO.

1 On-page means everything that's on the pages of your website; namely, your site's content. It's what you can most easily control.

2 Off-page is everything that Google could discover about your organization that's out in the greater internet. It's harder to control but not impossible.

3 Local SEO is all about making sure Google knows where you are, so you can be included in search results by customers and clients nearby.

There are no shortcuts. You need to give it time. I cannot stress this enough: although time is an unknown quotient, it makes all the difference. SEO is worth your efforts, but it can take awhile to come around. Think 18 months, not 18 days.

On-page SEO

As we discussed in the content chapter, the words, images, and video on your website need to attract your ideal customer. While it's important to always be thinking of them first, you should also consider how Google reads the content of your webpages too. To do this, we start by working backwards: begin with the moment someone searches.

What would your ideal client or customer be searching for in Google to find you? These words and phrases are called **keywords**, and for maximum SEO exposure, you need to know what keywords to prioritize. To do this, you can use the keyword toolbox from Google or similar sites (ads.google.com/intl/en_ca/home/tools/keyword-planner, kwfinder.com, moz.com/explorer). You can incorporate the words you find into your site, wherever they make sense. When you type in different words or phrases, you can see how many people search for those and closely matched terms, using different filters linked to who your audience is and what you're trying to achieve.

On your site, you have the opportunity to add keywords that match the interests of your audience. Be careful, though—search engines don't respond well to you adding every keyword you can think of. In fact, doing that will hurt your chances of being successful. Effective SEO means focusing in on a few key areas of interest and building an audience around those keywords rather than around all possibilities.

HERE'S HOW TO KEYWORD!

- Remember the power of "long-tail" keywords. Longer and more specific keyword phrases entered into the search bar are more likely to result in sales conversion because they will have lower competition in search engine results. No matter how hard you try, you're likely not going to have your small but mighty independent shoe boutique rank in the top 10 Google results for the keyword "shoes." The big guys have that locked down. You just can't compete! But you may be able to compete and rank higher for the keyword phrase "leather Oxford shoes handcrafted in Montreal."

- Sprinkle keywords and phrases throughout your website content, such as in your title tags, page titles, in the metadata and description, in headings, in your written copy, image tags, and your URL itself. Add them all over your site, not just on the homepage.

- Have a text hierarchy (Google loves headings, subheadings, and so on), and go top heavy with keywords in your paragraph headings as well as in the text itself.

- Be specific with keywords, especially including your local community and city in the phrases you use!

Off-page SEO

Google doesn't just look at your website itself when deciding how to rank it in search engine results. It also looks to a number of outside signals that tell it how trustworthy your website is. One of the strongest signals that the Google algorithm uses is the importance of links to your site. This part of the algorithm is called **PageRank**, and it measures both the quantity and quality of **inbound links**. This algorithm isn't only about numbers, which is why black-hat solutions are second rate.

Inbound links—links from other websites to yours—show Google that you're important, popular, and relevant. That drives you higher in search engine results. It *is* a popularity contest. The more that popular websites in the world link to your website, the more that Google thinks that you're popular. It's like high school. If you're the new kid in school, no one knows who you are. But if you go to the cafeteria at lunch and the most popular kid in school sits next to you, all of the sudden you're noticed. You're a hot commodity.

That's how PageRank works: you want to get other sites to link to your site. Google sees each inbound link as a vote for your page. The number of links and the value of each is a big factor in determining your rank. In general, if you want to show up in Google results above your competitors, you need to have a higher link value directed to each page you want to rank for.

Gaining links to your site is called **backlinking**, and it's an important part of your SEO efforts. Backlinks can be gained from link exchanges, forums, review sites, professional directory listings, presentation sites, coupon sites, press releases, social media, and other sources. A good place to start is to ask friends and family members to link their social media profiles, professional websites, and personal websites to your site, but you can go beyond that. Make a list of every place you think you could ask for a link to your website and reach out. Backlinking takes time and effort, but it's not super technical. This is most definitely something you can do yourself.

But remember! Not all links are equal. A link in a single tweet from Twitter isn't going to carry the same weight as a link from CNN.com. The more popular the site linking to you is, the more popular you look to Google. This is why so many people guest blog on other websites, hoping to score a high-value link back to their own site in the byline.

Local SEO

Remember before when I said that geographic location matters to search engines? It's true. Think about the last time you googled something local, like a dry cleaner or a pizza parlour. You were likely only delivered search results that were nearby. It makes sense if you think about it. Just because Joe's Pizza in Greenwich Village, New York, has one of the best slices of pizza pie you'll ever eat, that's not going to help you much when you're searching for pizza delivery and you're nowhere near New York City.

If you have a business that serves local customers or clients, let Google know so they can prioritize you in local search results. The best way to do this is to have a complete **Google My Business** profile.

Have you noticed that when searching for a business, Google will display a box with photos, maps, hours, contact info, and the organization's website? That's all information that you can submit to Google through the free Google My Business service. Go to Google.com/Business and complete all the sections. This is the number-one way to ensure that you appear correctly in local Google search results and Google Maps.

What about Google Ads?

If you are trying to build an audience, Google Ads can help quite a bit. With this service, people click your ad, which is based on your keywords and appears on the Google search pages that match them, and go to your website or call you directly. Best of all, you only pay when they click: the service is free until people actually click or complete an action that you specify ahead of time. We'll get into this more in chapter 10. The thing you need to know about Google Ads when it comes to SEO, however, is that they're totally separate. The only way, for example, that Google Ads can impact your Google ranking in organic search is that Google Ads can drive a lot of traffic to your site, and traffic is a popularity indicator.

So if you need an SEO boost in that department, Google Ads can help. But it's a short-term solution. The moment you stop driving traffic via Google Ads, your organic search positioning will adjust accordingly.

How I did it: The Camp Tech story

In the early days of Camp Tech, when we were an unknown entity in SEO land, I got an inkling that I needed to build some digital bridges. I paid a marketing assistant, who is now our director of marketing and sales, to work five hours a week to try to get links back to the Camp Tech website. We run workshops, so it made sense to post on event listing websites, but we also commented on blogs, asked to be included on professional directory websites, and contributed guest blog posts and articles to other sites, all so we could have a link back to Camp Tech's corner of the web. We created (and still create!) friendly partnerships with organizations that aren't competitors but appeal to similar target customers. How do we do it? We approach other organizations and ask if we can be "internet friends." What that means for our team, and for theirs, is that we'll amplify each other's messages on social media, in each other's email newsletters, and on each other's websites where appropriate. Camp Tech's SEO is really strong now as a result of the work we've put into this year in and year out.

What I love most about this is that it doesn't require any specific technical know-how. It just takes gumption, perseverance, a friendly attitude, and time!

Another digital marketing tactic we've used over the years is blogger and social media influencer outreach. Think about it. Many people purchase things, engage professional services, or seek out community help through recommendations from a friend, and bloggers and influencers can parallel these kinds of recommendations. This is because a blogger or social media influencer is an opinion leader in a specific demographic who can create word-of-mouth consumer interest. They may be seen as more credible than other types of media endorsements because they set standards for norms both within their peer group and for the broader public.

How do you reach a blogger or social media influencer and compel them to give you an inbound link? Here's a four-step plan.

1   **Explore the internet.** Start with a search of bloggers who work in your area and begin with those who are the most popular. Don't limit yourself to written blogs. Try YouTubers and podcasters as well: search YouTube and Apple Podcasts for the people who talk about the kinds of things that you do.

2   **Do your research.** Find out what interests your chosen bloggers or influencers have, and tailor an email of introduction to each of them. This is not time to send out a shotgun letter with the same information to each person. Ensure that you are aware of their aims and make sure your letter is appropriate.

3   **Connect.** Use an email or even send a handwritten note along and include a free sample of your work to bloggers or influencers who respond to your invitation to chat. Include your contact information, and mention that you're available for interviews. Consider offering to do a contest or giveaway. Bloggers and influencers love to run

contests because it attracts traffic to their sites and social media profiles, and if you provide the prize for a contest, it's win-win!

4 **Follow up.** Just like all of us, bloggers and influencers are under a lot of time pressure. Try to be patient and follow up with an email about a week later with a personalized thank-you note.

This has been an important tactic to build Camp Tech's SEO, whether it was an exchange of support for free coverage in blogs, or even paying money to bloggers or local listing websites to do this. We've paid anywhere between $100 and $2,000, and I've always thought it was money well spent, because I did the research and made sure it was the right opportunity before shelling out.

- Most bloggers will automatically provide a link to your website, so that you can drive up your SEO opportunities.

- Post links to the review on your website and social media.

- If you are provided with a video interview, make sure you get permission to copy the video to your site or YouTube account.

- Disclosure is important! Even if you're not paying a blogger or influencer to write about you, you need to disclose your relationship. Check out Ad Standards' Influencer Marketing Disclosure Guidelines (adstandards.ca/resources/library).

. . . .

CHAPTER 7 FROM 30,000 FEET

There's a clear formula for search engine optimization (SEO) and it takes time and effort. You can't trick Google and other search engines with black-hat SEO strategies.

. . . .

Search engines like Google take hundreds of factors into consideration when ranking websites in results pages.

. . . .

The three areas you can focus on to increase your search engine presence are:

→ on-page SEO, through optimizing your content to make your site more discoverable for keywords;
→ off-page SEO, using backlinking strategies; and
→ local SEO, using tools such as Google My Business.

. . . .

Developing Camp Tech's strong SEO presence took years of consistent effort, but it was worth it. Two big things we did to help were to:

→ partner with businesses (not competitors!) that appeal to similar target customers, and
→ connect with bloggers and social media influencers to create word-of-mouth consumer interest.

. . . .

8

Social Media

AFTER 11 YEARS of working for a major bank, Annie was bored, uninspired, and ready for a change. Her true love was baking, not banking. Annie was at her happiest making delicious (and beautiful) cupcakes for her friends and family. She daydreamed about quitting her day job and opening up a bake shop. It just seemed so risky, though!

Annie decided to make her move towards small business ownership in stages. She transitioned her role at the bank to a part-time position, so she could spend more time baking in the industrial kitchen she rented by the hour. Annie took orders from friends and friends of friends, and little by little word about her amazing cupcakes started to spread.

All the while, Annie shared her small business journey on a Facebook page she set up for her fledgling business.

She shared behind-the-scenes photos and videos of what she was making and wrote honestly about the ups and downs of entrepreneurship. It really resonated with her social media followers, resulting in a devoted community of fans.

After two years of working part-time at the bank and part-time in her bakery, Annie had built enough of a customer base to take the leap. She rented a storefront, left her job, and went all in on the bake shop. Annie attributes a lot of her early success to social media.

———————

SOCIAL MEDIA IS here to stay. In just over a decade, it's changed the way individuals interact with one another and the way companies do business, which means that it is reshaping the way we live and interact with one another. The impact of social media on modern communication cannot be overstated.

You can most definitely use social media to build your brand and get you closer to achieving your business goals, regardless of your organization's size. That's one of the key benefits of social media—it's a level playing field. Whether you're a small but mighty business or an international conglomerate, every social media account is equal, at least at the start. Everyone has the potential for greatness without having to spend money.

Social media is quirky, with its own rules and cultures. It moves fast and changes quickly. Most importantly, social media is supposed to be *social*. When you're thinking about it, and all the things you need to do to incorporate social media into your business or organization, *you have to be confident that you want to use it.* If you aren't excited about social media, it's not going to work.

Of course, it's important to go where your target audience is and be active on the platforms that they're active on. But if you don't enjoy a social media platform at least a little bit, it's going to feel like a chore, and you won't succeed there. You know the feeling when you're at a party that you just don't belong at and all you want to do is bail? That's what some social networks can feel like. Explore them to find the one that feels right for you and for your audience. Personally, I just can't get into LinkedIn. I know why it's important, and I know I could definitely grow my business there, but, to me, it's boring. It's not right for me, and even though I've tried a number of times, I don't feel social there. But you'll find me actively oversharing on Twitter and Instagram, where I feel right at home.

Which social media platform is right for you?

You can grow your reputation in your chosen social community wherever your potential audience lives.

We're going to go through all of the major platforms here and talk about who lives where and what it takes to be successful on each platform. Once we're through the list, you should have a better idea of where you should spend your time to grow your business on social media.

Facebook

As you probably know, Facebook is the largest social media network in the world. Users create a personal profile which they can link to their friends' profiles as well as to businesses, organizations, events, and other groups based on interests. They can also send messages and update their personal profiles to notify friends about themselves. In addition, users can join networks organized by a city, region, organization, and more.

Facebook stands out from other social media applications due to two things: the demographic extent of its overall usership and the fact that the majority of its users tend to turn to Facebook before any other social media platform at the present time.

- **Best audience:** Everyone. Seriously. Even though there's been recent chatter about people abandoning the platform, there are still billions of people who use it every day. Facebook's core audience does skew a bit older in demographics. The dominant age group on Facebook isn't teens and 20-somethings—they're more likely to be on Instagram or Snapchat (I don't recommend using Snapchat in a business context). But there are still plenty of teens and 20-somethings active on Facebook, as well as pretty much every other demographic.

- **Drawback:** Facebook's algorithm prioritizes content from friends and family, making it hard for updates from businesses to be seen. More on this later in this chapter.

- **How to get started:** You need a (free) personal Facebook profile to log in, and from there you can build a (free) company page.

- **Post frequency:** Post at least three times a week.

- **Companies using Facebook well, to inspire you:** Michelle Bridges 12 Week Body Transformation (facebook.com/ 12WBT), Seventh Generation (facebook.com/seventh generation), and Harry's Razors (facebook.com/hapo strophe).

YouTube

We're all familiar with YouTube—it's the social media network for video. And it's the second largest social site in the world, as well as the second largest search engine. It's a place where people can experiment with video and deliver new ways of seeing the world through the eyes of an individual, rather than through a corporate body such as a television studio or network. In this way, it's very creative. Best of all, when you create videos, people can get to know you better as an individual, which can be extremely beneficial to building your brand.

- **Best audience:** Millennials and younger audiences; niche audiences.

- **Drawback:** Making videos is hard!

- **How to get started:** Set up a free account, then make short, simple videos using your smartphone. The content of the video is more important than the production quality—audiences will forgive you if your video is shaky or your sound isn't perfect as long as what you're sharing is entertaining or educational.

- **Post frequency:** Post once a week.

- **Companies using YouTube well, to inspire you:** Sephora (youtube.com/sephora), Red Bull (youtube.com/redbull) and Expedia (youtube.com/expedia).

Twitter

Ah, Twitter. Even if you don't use it, you've probably heard of it. And you've probably been confused by Twitter—of all the major social media networks, it's the one with the most particular rules of engagement and unique-to-itself culture.

Some people (like me) love it, and some people hate it. Twitter is divisive, to say the least.

Twitter has been around for a while, and there was a time when Twitter was considered essential to a business's social media strategy. That's not the case anymore, as other social media networks have grown faster than Twitter in recent years. At the end of 2018, Twitter publicly said they had 321 million monthly active users worldwide. That's roughly 33 percent of Instagram's monthly active users from the same time and roughly 14 percent of Facebook's.

If your target audience is on Twitter, by all means, you should be there engaging with them. But if you're not totally sure, or you don't have the time that Twitter requires (it's the most time intensive of all the social networks listed here), then you have my permission to skip it.

- **Best audience:** Business leaders, journalists, politicos, Gen Xers, and older Millennials.

- **Drawback:** You have to post a lot (many times a day) and respond to replies and other's tweets. Twitter is all about engagement.

- **How to get started:** Set up a free account—there's no difference between personal and business accounts on Twitter.

- **Post frequency:** Post at least 20 times a week and log in to respond and retweet at least three times a day.

- **Companies using Twitter well, to inspire you:** Grammarly (twitter.com/grammarly), Wendy's (twitter.com/wendys), and Charmin (twitter.com/charmin).

LinkedIn

LinkedIn is professional networking in a social media context. Plus, it has job postings. LinkedIn leverages business contacts, where people can share thoughts with colleagues, as well as business information associated with individual corporations and organizations, such as slide decks and white papers. This site works really well if you're in a professional services field such as accounting, real estate, or the law, among others.

- **Best audience:** Business-to-business organizations, service businesses.

- **Drawback:** Very business focused; a bit dull.

- **How to get started:** Set up a free account for yourself, then build a page for your company.

- **Post frequency:** Post at least once a week, log in every or every other day to respond to others' posts.

- **Companies using LinkedIn well, to inspire you:** Jack Welch Management Institute (linkedin.com/school/the-jack-welch-management-institute), WeWork (linkedin.com/company/wework), and Tesla (linkedin.com/company/tesla-motors).

Instagram

The fastest growing of the social media juggernauts, Instagram is a social media site based on photography. If your work is at all visual, if you sell products, or if your target audience skews younger, this is a place for you to start. Your aim will be to capture and share images of things and ideas that represent your brand.

- **Best audience:** 68 percent female; Instagram is popular with 30- to 49-year-olds and very popular with teens and 18- to 29-year-olds.

- **Drawback:** You need strong visual content to share.

- **How to get started:** Sign up for a free business account.

- **Post frequency:** Post three to five times a week; daily in Instagram Stories.

- **Companies using Instagram well, to inspire you:** Starbucks (instagram.com/starbucks), Brit + Co (instagram .com/britandco), and the TSA—no joke, the Transportation Security Administration has a huge following on Instagram (instagram.com/tsa).

Pinterest

Pinterest is also a social media site based on photography but, arguably, it's more about community than business. What do I mean by that? Well, as a business you can definitely have a Pinterest page and post the same kinds of images that you would on Instagram, as well as direct product shots. But what happens with those images is that people collect them. Pinning an image, to your audience, is about adding it to a specific group of other images that inspires them. Pinterest can be huge for SEO (as it can drive more traffic to your website than any other social media platform) and for building buzz for visual brands. This is a great platform for product companies and those who want to inspire a community.

- **Best audience:** 81 percent of Pinterest users are women; Millennials are the most active on the platform.

- **Drawback:** You need images to participate.

- **How to get started:** Sign up for a free business account.

- **Post frequency:** Log in at least once daily to pin and participate in group boards.

- **Companies using Pinterest well, to inspire you:** HomeAway (pinterest.com/homeaway), West Elm (pinterest.com/westelm), and Ziploc (pinterest.com/ziplocofficial).

Choose wisely

Even if one of these platforms appeals the most, you may want to experiment with a number of different social platforms to see what works for you. It could change over time, so feel free to play and test.

But, before you really dig in, you have to remember one thing. Do not participate in any social media platform you're not going to commit yourself to. If you find that a social media platform isn't working for you—you're not enjoying it, it feels like a chore, and it's not helping you achieve your business goals—then go ahead and quit it. The only thing I ask you not to do is leave a bunch of social media "zombie accounts" around the internet. What do I mean by "zombie accounts"? They're not dead, but they're certainly not alive. It's better to delete an account and not be on a particular social media channel than it is to let an account stagnate.

What to post on social media

Social media is a hungry beast. It eats content with a voracious, never-ending appetite. "I don't know what to post" is the most common refrain I hear from small business owners when it comes to social media.

Okay, so what do you actually post on social media? I don't know exactly where it came from, but I do like the 80/20 rule. The 80/20 rule says that approximately 80 percent of what you post on social media should be social and 20 percent should be promotional in nature. Remember social media is social, first and foremost. Even though businesses are on social media, the ones that succeed develop a brand voice that is very human. You can be funny, kind, enthusiastic, goofy, empathetic, casual, even snarky if you want, but be human. Messages that are robotic, stilted, or stiff don't resonate.

15 ideas for social media content

If you're drawing a blank on *exactly what* to share on social media, here are 15 ideas that can get the creative juices flowing.

1   **Link to your own content.** This is the obvious stuff for sharing on social media—your content is created to be shared! If you're making any of the content we talked about in chapter 6 (things like blog posts, podcast episodes, or videos), then share it often on social.

2   **Contests and giveaways.** Who doesn't love a contest or giveaway? This works really well if you sell a product and can give away samples online, but even if you don't have physical goods, you can do a social media contest. If it's appropriate for your line of work, give away an hour's worth of your service. Or make some fun promotional items with your company's logo on them and give those away through an online contest. Can't think of anything to

give away? A gift card is always a safe bet. You'd be amazed at what people will do to enter a contest for a $25 coffee shop gift card. Important legal reminder: online contests and giveaways need terms and conditions, and you'll need to check with gaming laws in your region.

3   **Gift guides and wish lists.** This idea works well for product businesses (make a list of top picks for an upcoming holiday and be sure to put your product on the list among others). Include images and it can be used as a carousel of photos on Instagram or a list with links on Facebook. Make it into a collage and post to Pinterest!

4   **Behind-the-scenes look at your biz.** Everyone loves a peek behind the curtain. Take a few photos or even write a couple sentences about what you're working on today, and post that to social media. It shows personality and authenticity when you're being real with your clients and customers.

5   **Stats, data, and trends.** If you have access to industry stats or data, you can share that for interested clients or customers (especially on LinkedIn, which is very business focused). Don't limit yourself to industry-wide info, though—if you've noticed something specific in your own business, share it. For example, are sales of a particular product much higher than they were this time last year? That's a trend, and your social media followers might find that super interesting to learn.

6   **User-generated content.** User-generated content is a clunky marketing term for reposting or sharing what others have posted about you. It's hands down one of

the most effective social media content ideas because a) it requires almost no effort on your part, and b) it makes the person who first posted the message feel special to be called out. This works really well on Instagram and Twitter, where you can repost or retweet someone's message—and add your own "thanks so much for mentioning us" note to it.

7   **#ThrowbackThursday or #FlashbackFriday posts.** #ThrowbackThursday (also known as #TBT) and #FlashbackFriday (a.k.a. #FBF) are common hashtags on Instagram, Facebook, and Twitter, where people share old photos on Thursdays or Fridays. Find a photo or a video of something you were doing awhile ago (even a year or a few months ago is fine—it doesn't have to be ancient history). Save it for a Thursday or Friday, and then post it with a caption explaining what it was and add the hashtag #ThrowbackThursday, #TBT, #FlashbackFriday, or #FBF.

8   **How-to or instructional posts.** How-to videos are some of the most popular on YouTube and there's a good reason why: they're practical and helpful. Make a short video showing how to use one of your products, or a quick explainer of how a particular part of your service business works.

9   **Go live with a Q&A or AMA.** Facebook, Instagram, Twitter, and YouTube each has the ability for you to host a live, interactive video chat with your followers. You can do this spontaneously or plan to do a live video and announce it ahead of time. If people know to join you, you can use the

time to do a question and answer session or an AMA ("ask me anything").

10   **Feature members of your team.** I love this idea because it's great behind-the-scenes content and it's also great for company morale. Do a whole series of social media posts featuring photos and fun information about each of your team members.

11   **Spotlight on loyal customers or clients.** This is similar to the concept above, but this time, shine the spotlight on some of your favourite or most loyal customers or clients. Ask them for a photo or take a photo of them using your product or visiting you in your office. Share it with their name and a short story about why you love having them as your client. Not only will it make that person a super-fan who will tell everyone they know, it shows your other social media followers that you care about your customers.

12   **Quotes and testimonials from customers or clients.** Speaking of your customers and clients, ask them for quotes or testimonials. Or, if someone leaves a great review of your business on Google Reviews or Yelp (or some other ratings or reviews platform), you can definitely share that on social media. Either take a screenshot of the review, or copy and paste the quote into a simple graphic design program and make your own image of the testimonial.

13   **Poll your audience or start a quiz.** Social media polls or quizzes can be a lot of fun. Twitter and Instagram Stories

have a poll function built in. Launching a new product or service? Poll your social media audience for their opinions. You can also make a poll that's tied to a pop culture event, such as which team you hope will win the World Series, or what movie you should watch on the weekend. Instagram Stories has quiz functionality as well.

14   **Share a milestone.** This is similar to the behind-the-scenes idea, but this one focuses specifically on a milestone. It's okay to toot your horn if you do so in an authentic, grateful way. Celebrating your fifth year of business? Recently opened a second location? Share it, and thank your community for supporting you along the way.

15   **Find other businesses to amplify on social media.** This idea comes from Camp Tech—it's the "internet friends" concept I described in chapter 7. It's a strategy we used to grow our social media presence in the early days, and we still use it now to keep growing. We made a list of organizations that target the same type of customer that we do but we aren't in direct competition with. We followed them on social media, repeatedly liking and sharing what they were posting. By amplifying their message to our followers, we did them a favour. Before long, they noticed and returned the favour. It's a great way to cross-pollinate your marketing messages with another organization.

Social media culture and etiquette

After "I don't know what to post," the second most common refrain I hear from small business owners on social media is "I don't have time to think of different content to post on different social media platforms. Can't I just post the same message everywhere?"

I'm sorry, friends, but you can't. Think of each social media platform like a party, each with its own culture and etiquette. You wouldn't wear a tuxedo to a beach bonfire party, and you wouldn't wear a bathing suit and cut-offs to a gala dinner. To that end, the kind of content that works well on Instagram won't fly on Twitter, and the kind of content that works well on Twitter won't resonate on LinkedIn. Read the room and know what's appropriate for each context. You can most definitely post the same general message on more than one social media platform, but tweak the tone, presentation, and details of the post to suit the situation.

Cross-posting from platform to platform is another no-no. What do I mean by cross-posting? It's when you make a post somewhere (say, Instagram) and then you set the system to automatically push out the same message on another social platform (say, Twitter). Sounds like a time saver, right? I'm all for time savers, but this one doesn't look good on you. It shows that you're not really "in the room." An Instagram post that's cross-posted to Twitter will include a link to Instagram inside the tweet. That forces people to click, leave Twitter, go to Instagram, see your post, and then go back to Twitter. Asking your audience to leave one platform and go to another just to see your message is asking too much—especially when you won't do it yourself. If you want to share on Twitter, go to Twitter and share there. Don't stand in the Instagram room and yell into the Twitter room, "Hey! I'm over here!"

And while we're on the subject of time savers, let's talk about social media automation. Using social media tools to schedule posts you've written is one thing (more on that in a minute) but using bots to post automatically generated messages is another. Here's an example of what I'm talking about. Have you ever followed someone new on Instagram or Twitter and immediately received a DM (direct message) that says, "Hey! Let me introduce myself" or something like that? Odds are it was a pre-populated message set to automatically send to new followers. While it's definitely a nice idea to say hello and introduce yourself, sending a robotic message to do it for you is definitely not nice. If you wouldn't do that in the real world, why does it seem okay to do it online? Automated messages are gross, and I recommend avoiding them.

If you don't have something nice to say...

You don't *have* to be nice on social media, but it is certainly a safe bet for most businesses, unless it's part of your brand to be cynical or irreverent. And, of course, even if you are nice, not everyone else will be. What do you do if someone says something negative to you online? First up, do not delete their comment, and do not fire back! Acknowledge what they're saying and respond professionally.

It's not a bad idea to compile a set of social media guidelines for everyone in your organization. It's especially helpful to have a social media guideline document if you have more than one person posting on behalf of your business. Creating one doesn't have to be a huge undertaking. Write up a short list of words and phrases you do and don't use, with examples of things your company would or wouldn't say online. Add to it as you go. Before you know it, you'll have a policy document that everyone can refer to.

Social media management tools

Writing, posting, and responding to social media can feel like a full-time job (and for some people, it is!). There are a few tools that can help make you more efficient and organized as you slay the social beast.

I'm a big fan of editorial content calendars. They don't need to be fancy—a spreadsheet is all you need. Make a column for each social media platform you want to post to and make rows for day and time. Then start populating the spreadsheet with content. I like to write about a week's worth of posts at a time, and I find if I brew a fresh cup of coffee, sit and put my head down, I can get it done in about an hour. You can work collaboratively with a co-worker on your content calendar if that helps. The key point here is to set aside time to write your social media content, so you have it ready to go when you need it.

Whether or not you should then schedule your content is a divisive subject among social media professionals. Personally, I'm on team schedule. I don't mind scheduling social media posts because, for so many small businesses I know, that's the only way the messages are going to get out. You can use a social media management tool like Sprout Social, Buffer, or Hootsuite to log in to all your accounts in one centralized place and set messages to go out at a scheduled future time from there. For many small business owners, myself included, the ability to write social media posts in advance and then go into a tool and schedule them makes all the difference. I have two important notes for you about scheduling social media posts.

1   Scheduling posts does not replace interaction on social media platforms. You still need to log in to each platform

you're on at least once a day (if not two or three times a day) to respond to comments on your posts and to respond to what other people are posting.

2   Be mindful of what's going on in the world. If there's a natural disaster or some other catastrophe, go into your scheduling tool and pause your posts from going out. Many people use social media to communicate information in a crisis, and it's important to "keep the lines clear." Promotional posts about your business do not belong next to essential news items, and if you have scheduled messages going out during an emergency, you could be criticized harshly for being insensitive.

CAUTION! THE SOCIAL MEDIA TRAP

OFTEN PEOPLE GET so excited and wrapped up in the social part of social media, that they only end up "talking" to their friends or other people who aren't really their target audience. And they get so obsessed with how their social media is going that they not only lose time, but they follow the wrong metrics (or not bother to measure how they're doing at all). I often see business owners on social media who aren't going anywhere. They're posting a lot and trying to reach people and generate engagement on the platforms, but it has little or no effect. They're like someone treading water: they're moving their arms and legs (and are likely exhausted from the effort), but they're no closer to the shore. Social media can be a beautiful distraction, but after a long time of treading water, if you don't reach the shore, you drown.

You can most definitely build a business using social media, but you need to pay attention to how you're doing and whether your social media efforts are actually getting you closer to your business goals. The metrics and measurements inside social media analytics are not there for your vanity. Focus on them to build your business, not your ego.

Social media measurement

Of all the digital marketing options at your disposal, I find social media the hardest to measure in terms of impact. It can be really difficult to see a direct correlation between a single tweet and a sale. That's because a customer or client often has to go through a process of getting to know your business before making a purchasing decision. That process takes them from first becoming aware of your brand, to learning more and engaging with you, to converting to a customer. It usually requires them to interact with you a few times (for example, by visiting your website, receiving an email newsletter, or seeing a message on social media).

One of the hardest parts of measuring the impact of digital marketing is attribution: the ability to correctly attribute a sale to the marketing channel that caused it. Sure, you can look at referral data that tells you what link someone clicked before making a purchase. But if someone clicks a link to your website from Facebook and goes on to purchase something on your site, that doesn't mean that the effort spent on Facebook posts is 100 percent responsible for that sale. The customer could have done a Google search and visited your website a few weeks ago, or they talked to a friend over coffee and your business name came up, and finally they saw the Facebook post that they clicked on. It's hard to give credit where credit is due, since tracking is an incomplete science. But, more often than not, a customer or client has heard about you or interacted with your business more than once before you make that sale.

That's why, when it comes to social media measurement, it's important to look beyond conversion metrics. Of course, conversion (the moment someone converts to a customer or client, a.k.a. a sale or purchase or inquiry) is very important, but it's not the only thing that can be measured. With social media measurement, we're often looking at indicators that someone is on their way to converting. And there are certain metrics that are best used to indicate where someone is in their customer journey. We'll take a deeper look at this in chapter 11.

. . . .

CHAPTER 8 FROM 30,000 FEET

Social media is a great low-cost and low-tech tool for building a small business, but it moves fast and has its own rules and culture.

. . . .

It's very difficult to be on all social media channels. Discover where your target audience is and pick one or two channels to participate in, based on where your people are.

. . . .

If you need inspiration to get your creative juices flowing, try my 15 ideas for social media content.

. . . .

Social media etiquette is important. Don't cross-post
between platforms or send automated responses.
Consider creating a social media guideline document
for your business.

. . . .

Use editorial calendars and scheduling tools to make
social media management easier.

. . . .

When measuring social media impact, remember to
focus on your KPI, not vanity metrics.

. . . .

9

Email Marketing

THERE ARE SEASONS to most businesses—times of the year when they are busier than others, or times when they spend more effort on certain aspects of their business, like planning or execution. For Tim, the owner of a small landscaping business, there are literal seasons to consider. From spring to mid-autumn, Tim is doing what he loves most: getting his hands dirty and turning his client's properties from "meh" to "wow."

But in the winter, the phone doesn't ring much. That's why Tim relies on email marketing as a prime way to stay in touch with past, current, and prospective clients. He's grown his recipient list over time, collecting email addresses through an email signup form on his website and a link to sign up at the bottom of every landscaping estimate he sends out.

His emails are helpful with tips on how to care for a garden year-round and include photos of stunning landscapes to get people excited for the upcoming planting season. Tim's customers know that his emails are helpful and inspirational. They know when they open an email from Tim, they'll go on a beautiful journey into a lush landscape, even when there's two feet of snow on the ground outside.

EMAIL MARKETING IS old school... and it works.

One of the only digital marketing channels that can directly target your customer or client, email marketing is a solid choice for getting your message across.

Oh, I know you're probably doubting me right now. You have that skeptical look on your face because, well, you're personally tired of all of the emails from a hotel chain in your inbox that you don't remember signing up for, or the multiple invitations you're getting to that self-help seminar on the California coast that costs more than your car. But the reason you're getting all of those emails is the proof in the pudding: they work.

Email marketing doesn't require a lot of tech know-how, and it's one of the most cost-effective digital marketing methods you can invest in. That means that you're likely going to get a high return on your investment of time and money. It's even less of a commitment to manage an email campaign than a social media campaign. You don't have to keep pushing out a new message every day or spend time looking through comments, shares, and likes.

This is all great, but hands down, the best thing about email marketing and building your email list is that it's yours.

For many industries, an email list is a serious business asset, the kind that is considered when determining the value of a company. It's that important. You own your email marketing list. It will never belong to your email host, your website host, or anyone else. That means you can export it and take it to a different email service or system whenever you want.

But just like any other digital marketing endeavour in this book, you're going to have to start with a strategy to make sure that your email marketing is working for you and aligned with your business goals.

In this chapter, we'll talk about developing an email list and what that means for you: professionally, legally, and strategically. We'll talk about how to manage email campaigns, open rates, clickthrough rates, and conversion, and something marketing pros call your most desired response (MDR): helping you get your clients to do the one thing you want them to do, as often as possible.

Finally, we'll talk about what your customers want to get out of your email communication so, like you, they don't feel inundated and tune out. Just like everything else in the business world, there's always room to do better than other companies and organizations, and I've got a few tricks up my sleeve.

Strategy, once again

Where does email marketing fit within your overall digital marketing strategy?

Let's start with your most desired response (MDR).

What's the purpose of your marketing email? Is it to inform your client of something about your product or service (such as where to buy it, so they can do just that!), to persuade them of something (such as the value of your work, so they want to hire you), or to get them to do something (such as purchase something or talk about it with friends)?

The answers to these questions will determine the kind of content you'll be sending out.

If your MDR is to get someone to buy something, then you have to figure out why they ought to buy something now, rather than later. Are you having a sale or promotion? Are you introducing new products or a new service? Are you opening a new location near them? Are you planning to bundle some products to get people in the door, like offering a free book when someone attends your next speaker series? The trick is to determine what benefit your client is going to get when they open the email. Always be thinking: *Why would my reader want this email? What value is it to them? Why should they care?* Make it clear and easy for someone to see the benefit in your email campaigns, and they'll look forward to receiving them.

How do you determine an MDR that's not "to sell a product"? What if you're trying to promote services or educate your readers? It's not all that different. The key to success is still in the "what's in it for me?" approach. With a product-based email promotion, you can easily have a sale. That will motivate your readers to make a purchase, which is likely your MDR. But financial savings aren't the only thing that your target customer or client could value, and making a sale isn't the only MDR you can use email marketing for. Email campaigns can be used to persuade clients of a new idea or of the value of your work.

What your people want to know, however, is *why* they should take the time to scan through *your* email out of the hundreds they will likely receive that week. You want to make the read valuable, rather than a throwaway. What can you share with them that will keep them onside? Are you thinking about having an event? Sharing some research your team has completed? What's newsworthy for your clients?

No matter what your aim, you need a general idea of what people are going to receive from you *before* you start that mailing list. Why?

Well, remember when we talked about GDPR and all of the other legislation around marketing communications with your customers? This is where it really matters. You need to let people know what to expect when they sign up for your email list (we'll get to that in a second), and you have to keep your word. People must consent to being on your list, and if they are bombarded with emails that don't have anything to do with what they signed up for, that's on you, both ethically and legally.

Let's quickly review the bottom line on the legal terms of engagement. Canada's Anti-Spam Legislation (CASL) requires consent (either implied or express consent) to send out emails to individuals. Express consent is easy—it's permission that someone gives you, either in writing or orally, to email them. Implied consent is trickier.

The law acknowledges that when people inquire about or make a purchase, they're engaging with your business. This is enough reason to add someone to your email list, even if they didn't expressly opt in. That's why, in some cases, when you buy something from a company and provide them with your email address to verify the transaction, you start receiving their newsletters or sales emails. Two very important things to note here: implied consent in Canada is time limited; it expires after two years. Also, implied consent is only valid under CASL, not under other laws. So if your email marketing list has people on it outside Canada, implied consent might not fly as a good enough reason to have them on your list.

The law that governs the European Union, the General Data Protection Regulation (GDPR), requires explicit consent to receive email marketing messages, and this is the way that laws in other parts of the word are heading too. What "explicit consent" means is that they need to sign themselves up for the list or give you specific permission orally ("Please sign me up for your email list"). You need to keep records that people have given this consent. There is no equivalent to implied consent in the GDPR.

Under some laws (like CASL), you may be able to add your entire customer database to your email marketing list, even if they haven't explicitly opted in. But email marketing, like a lot of digital marketing really, is a quality over quantity game. I'd rather you have 300 people on your email marketing list that are super engaged with what you have to say, versus 300,000 people on your list who don't even open your messages. It's why I would think twice before blanketing everyone you've ever met with promotional emails. No one likes spam. Not only is it annoying for your email recipient, it's also bad business. Blasting a message to a big email list without any sense of who you're talking to and what they want to hear is what I refer to as a "spray and pray" mentality. It is much less likely to drive sales than a more measured, targeted approach, and it can also backfire. If your message is considered "spammy" by an email provider, it will end up not only in the spam folder of your recipient's email inbox but also in the spam folders of others who use the same email provider. Then your message won't even be seen, which is the exact opposite of what you're trying to achieve.

The best clients and customers are those who really want to hear from you. Some people scoff at permission-based email marketing, but in my books, it's the best form of email marketing.

Email marketing is a match game. It's not about blasting home a single message to everyone in the world; it's about finding connections between people, opportunities, and outcomes that work. That's why the law, as it is evolving, really does match your strategy more than you think. You want the right people in the room so that what you have to say matters, and you want to give them the information they need to make decisions that are of mutual benefit. You're building the framework for a win-win so that everyone is happy.

Who wants to hear from you? More people than you'd think

How will you get people to sign up for your email mailing list? The same way that you've gotten people involved in your business in the past: find them, engage with them, and then ask for their contact details. Here are a few places that you may or may not have considered.

- Put signup forms everywhere. Okay, maybe not *everywhere*, but you can have more than one on your website and in other places beyond your website. Think about where people look for your information. Do you have a storefront or use posters for advertising in real life? Make sure your contact information and website are well placed and large enough to read. Are you having an event or tradeshow? Use an email signup sheet at your booth, at the door, or by the cash bar.

- Be super social. Consider putting a link to your email signup form in the email signature of your normal biz correspondence ("Join our mailing list to receive exclusive promotions monthly") and place a few posts on your social media once in a while ("We have a great email newsletter about permaculture and home gardens going out tomorrow morning—are you on the list to receive it? Sign up here").

- Optimize your website signups. Consider putting an email signup on every page (say, in the footer or on the top right of the site) and also a more prominent email signup on a few select pages (such as the contact page). Even the homepage is a great place to collect email addresses. Try using a signup box somewhere prominent (with a short but clear indication of what people will receive, right there in the box).

- To pop up or not to pop up? Pop-up messages on websites with prompts to sign up for a list can be an effective way to collect email addresses, but they can also be really annoying, especially if they keep reappearing or are difficult to close! If you're going to do a pop-up message, make sure:

  → It's easy to dismiss, using a single click.
  → It's mobile friendly; there's nothing worse than getting a pop-up on your smartphone that you can't close it because it takes up the whole screen.
  → It's enticing; you're interrupting someone in the middle of browsing your website, so it better be worth it. Offer a special promo code or discount for signing up, or a high-value download like a tip sheet or white paper.

→ You monitor it and get rid of it if needed. If a pop-up has been on your site for a few weeks and you've only received one or two signups even though your website traffic is in the hundreds, it's not working. Kill it.

Wherever you have your email signup form, whether online or in person, be sure to tell people what to expect. As we've talked about, a simple "join our email list" or "sign up for our email newsletter" isn't going to cut it. Tell people *why* they should sign up and be clear about what they're going to get. "Sign up for our weekly email newsletter for information about upcoming workshops and secret sales" is much more convincing. While every email must have an obvious way to opt out or unsubscribe—so that people who aren't a good match for your content get to run for the hills if they so choose—your clients will feel more secure in making the decision to connect with you in the first place if they understand what they are going to get out of your future communications.

SHOULD YOU SEGMENT YOUR LIST?

WHILE IT'S TOTALLY fine to send one message to all of your email recipients, sending targeted messages to specific segments of your list can result in higher email open and clickthrough rates. And you have to think about this ahead of time, not just at the last moment when your email is about to go out, because segmentation is all about collecting the right information about your clients in the first place.

Can you group your email list into sections of recipients based on their relationship with your organization? Do you need to target different parts of the country or world, where there are different time zones? And would you want to send different messages to those groups, or schedule them to receive information at different times?

Think about what information you need to collect directly from your clients (home address? interests?) and what you can collect from your store or event systems (purchase history? attendance records?) in order to achieve your goals.

What goes in the email?

What kind of content do you want to offer your readers? For service businesses, you're likely trying to build your reputation as an expert. A newsletter, or a "letter from the desk of," can help you pique your readers' interest in new ideas in your field. Links to industry articles you've read, along with your comments, can help to establish you as an expert who matters. Short excerpts from blog posts (if you have a blog) with a link to the full post can also be included in a newsletter. Make sure you use images if you're trying to garner interest in something that has a visual impact, like a forest restoration project or a new architectural design.

For product businesses, new or seasonal item launches are always a good bet for customers who are regulars. People want to see what's new in stock, especially if you have eye-catching new colours and styles to share. Sales and promotions, such as contests and giveaways, are always welcome and will likely result in a high clickthrough rate. "Abandoned cart" emails target people who have started a purchase process but not yet completed it; you can do this when you create links between your store software and your email strategy, and when people are already customers in your store system.

For all types of businesses, events are a great way to engage in email marketing, especially once people have signed up to your newsletter. You can use your email system to manage not only the selling of tickets for an event but for follow-up emails and event coordination for those who are going to attend, such as lists of what to bring, what to expect, and scheduling. Doing this well, and pointing emails back to resources on your site, can solidify your reputation with your audience over the long term and help them perceive your website as a resource.

Think like an email recipient

Think about what kind of promotional or informational emails you get that you actually enjoy receiving. Why do you like them? What makes you open them? I bet it's because they make you *feel* something. Perhaps you read a comedy newsletter because you find it funny and it brightens your day. Or you read an email from your favourite store because you have VIP status there (which makes you feel special and exclusive). Local news emails make you feel informed (and maybe even a bit smug when you are the smartest person in the room at your next dinner party). A service business might send helpful tips that ease the pain of a professional challenge you've been facing. Remember this when you're crafting your own email campaigns. Save your readers from boring or sales-y messages. The best marketing campaigns resonate because they make their readers feel something. Remember this is all about giving your readers something they value! Here's a list of some email marketing messages I enjoy receiving and why.

1   Weekly top 20 travel deal emails from Travelzoo (travel zoo.com). I look forward to receiving the Travelzoo emails every week. I know when to expect it (Wednesdays at exactly 12:09 p.m.) and I enjoy looking through the list of deals for local and distance travel they curate, usually when I'm taking a work break for lunch. The value for me is in the curation: Travelzoo combs a bunch of different websites, finding the top 20 deals. This saves me a bunch of time, something I really value.

2   Daily news roundup emails. I subscribe to a few of these, but my favourites are the ones that curate the news from a bunch of different sources and present it in an easily digestible way. My favourites are theSkimm (theskimm .com) which comes out in the morning, and Dave Pell's NextDraft (nextdraft.com) which comes out around 4 p.m. each day. Again, the value to me is in the curation and the consistency.

3   Flash sale emails. I'm pretty loyal to a Canadian airline called Porter, mostly for the flexibility they offer me to change flights without penalty (I'm a frequent flyer). Porter (flyporter.com) sends email messages with access to exclusive flash sales for their email subscribers. The

value is clear: these emails save me money. They do it so often that I will often wait for one before booking a flight. Depending on which way you look at it, that can be a good thing or a bad thing. Run too many promotions and you've created a culture of customers expecting sales. But if it drives people to purchase, maybe it's not such a bad thing in the end. Just be sure that the sale price still has room for profit; you don't want your customers to become addicted to sales where you lose money.

Email services that can help

Like everything else we've discussed so far, there are some quick ways to get started with email marketing so that you're not reinventing the wheel.

Yes, you can simply send marketing emails out from your regular email outbox, but if you do so, you're missing out on some of the most powerful (and legally acceptable) tools out there. Email marketing services allow you to prep everything seamlessly and within the legal parameters of the countries in which your clients live. They provide easy access to statistics to tell you how many people opened your emails, whether they clicked on the links in these emails, and when. These services are a great way to keep track of where you're doing well and where you can improve.

There are many different email marketing services, such as Constant Contact, Campaign Monitor, Litmus, Drip, AWeber, ConvertKit, and more. I personally prefer Mailchimp. We'll talk about them in a second. That being said, everything you're trying out in this chapter can apply to any email marketing platform, and I encourage you to find the best fit for your organization.

No matter what service you use, you have to remember one important thing. *Mobile-first thinking for email marketing is essential.* The majority of email is opened on a smartphone first, not on a desktop or laptop computer. Sure, someone might open an email on their phone and then open it again when they're at home or at the office on their computer. But there's a high likelihood your email marketing campaign is being viewed on a smartphone, and it needs to look good for that. You need to make sure that reading the email on a mobile device is a pleasant experience.

So, why do I think Mailchimp is the go-to resource for email marketing for small business? It's affordable, first and foremost. Mailchimp has a "forever free" plan where you can have up to 2,000 subscribers on your list and send out a whopping 12,000 emails per month, i.e., six emails to each of those 2,000 folks, for free (more at mailchimp.com/pricing). CASL, GDPR, and all other best practices are supported. That means that the system triggers you to include your full contact information and manages opt-in and opt-out processes for your subscribers instantaneously. They have mobile design covered, and they have features for advanced users that can scale with your organization's needs. Best of all, they have an easy-to-use web interface and an excellent support team, which means that you can get help when you want it.

Okay, let's get started

You've had a think about your strategy and your email's most desired response (MDR). Those are the broad strokes, and they are going to shape your next email or series of emails to your audience.

Here are the four questions that you need to ask yourself before actually putting the words together for your next campaign.

1   **Which business goal is this email supporting?** How am I going to further my strategy by sending out this message to people who are interested in my products or services?

2   **What is the number-one message I want to convey in the email?** What is my MDR right now, and do I have any additional messages that will help people say yes to my proposition? For example, if I want people to buy my ebook, could I give them access to a password-protected video series or podcast? If I want them to buy one of the dresses in my new spring collection, could I give them a subscriber discount?

3   **What value does the email bring to the reader?** Why should your reader care about the email? What will encourage them to open it in the first place, and how will it help them? What will they find valuable in the email—a sale or promotion, exclusive content they can't find anywhere else, a tip that they need to make their life easier, or a story to make them laugh or brighten their day?

4   **How will I measure the effectiveness of the email?** Is it only my MDR that I'm tracking? What else do I want to know? If people aren't following the MDR trail, it may be because the subject line of the email isn't getting them to open it. That will result in a poor *open rate*. It may be that the text in the email isn't compelling enough for them to click a link to purchase, which is called the *clickthrough*

rate. Conversion is the point at which you actually get your client to do what you wanted them to do (your MDR). You may want to think about what metric matters to you most: is it open rate, clickthrough rate, or conversion?

Test, test, test

What's the best time of day to send an email newsletter? What's the best day of the week? Which subject lines generate the most opens?

My honest professional advice: be like Goldilocks. Just like Goldilocks had to try three different types of porridge to see which one was "just right," you will not know what's right for you until you try a few different options. It's okay to not know until you try! Send one message at one time of day, send another message at another time of day, and then compare the results to see which one is "just right."

A lot of best practices in email timing depend on where you are, where your customers are, and who they are. Think about it. If you're a busy professional, and you receive a ton of advertising emails overnight, where do they go? If you're like me, they end up in the trash first thing, because you don't have time to read through them when you have more important emails to sort and respond to right away. I'm more likely to open an email if it comes during one of my lull times. Think coffee breaks: between 10 and 11 a.m. or between 2 and 3 p.m. is when I'm most likely to have a breather and see what people have to tell me.

Also consider: Is your business local or national? International? You may want to segment your clients by location so that they get your emails during the right time of day for their time zone. It may be worthwhile waiting for the right day of the week, often Tuesday through Thursday, to capture your audience. Wait until Friday afternoon and it will definitely get lost in the shuffle!

Most email marketing platforms also allow you to do A/B testing. What this means is that you can send out an email with different variants, like two different subject lines, to portions of your list to see which one performs better. In your A email—if you run a florist company, for example— you can try a creative subject line, like, "April showers bring May flowers," whereas in your B email you might try "15 percent off all floral arrangements in May." Then you see which email performs better, in this case, receiving a higher open rate than the other one. By using A/B testing, you can get a glimpse into the minds of your clients: do they respond to more creative or more financial incentives? Testing allows you to challenge your assumptions, and those of best-practice marketing gurus, to find out who your clients *really* are. Even if you don't do formal A/B testing, try a few different email formats, subject line styles, times and days of the week to send, and then compare the performance of those emails by looking at your metrics. What worked best for you?

And remember it has to look good too.

Earlier on, we talked about having your emails mobile-friendly. Before you send your email out, send a test email to yourself or to a colleague and open it on a mobile device. Are the images massive—do they need to be scaled down or cropped? Is the type readable? Are any sections of information displayed in side-by-side columns (which are hard to read on a small screen) instead of stacked rows? Do you have to "pinch and zoom" to read any part of the message, or is it all easily accessed by scrolling?

Mailchimp has a number of templates that include suggestions for fonts, colours, and styles that will work in every platform, from laptop to tablet to phone. You don't want to change these up too much: not every computer or smartphone works seamlessly with every font, for example, and choosing the wrong one can make your message literally unreadable. Programs like Mailchimp do the heavy lifting for you, so you don't have to worry.

Campaigning for the outcome you want

How do you know your email marketing is effective? Start with a goal for the email before you send it out. Of course, as I've been drilling home through this whole book, your strategy for your email marketing always ought to align with one of your business goals. That way you can determine the corresponding metric for measuring whether the email was successful or not. So, no matter what you are going to do, have a reason for doing it. None of us have time to waste on managing a communications campaign with a fuzzy rationale.

Once you have defined your goal, think about what matters to you and map out your measurement plan. Most email marketing platforms give you basic stats such as open rate, clickthrough rate, and unsubscribe information.

The **open rate** is a good indicator of the health of your email marketing campaign, but it's often not the *key* indicator of success. Why is that? Well, it's only step one in the process. The open rate is a great way to tell if you're creating wonderful subject lines, though. If you're getting a high open rate, you're doing a good job there, in matching your customer's sensibilities for what matters.

More often than not, the way to measure success of an email marketing campaign is the **clickthrough rate**. Did people click the link you were hoping they would? If not, they may not have been inspired by the copy in your email. Think about how to develop content that appeals to them. What can you do to engage them further?

If you have a high clickthrough rate, how many **sales or actions** did you achieve as the result of your campaign? If you got your clients all the way to your website and they didn't achieve your MDR, think about what barriers they may encounter there.

Your email marketing platform should be able to tell you who opened an email, at what time, what device they were on, and where they clicked. If your clients are on smartphones most of the time, it may be important to simplify the process as much as possible to accommodate for a small screen and longer load times.

But you won't know whether or not any of this information is valid unless you test, retest, and then try again.

A good way to get deeper information is to connect your email marketing platform to your website. This is another reason why I like Mailchimp, because it has so many integrations with website platforms. You can connect Mailchimp to most websites through integrations, and you can connect it to any site's Google Analytics account. We'll talk more about Google Analytics in chapter 11.

When everything is aligned, you can follow your client's click from your email to your website and track their behaviour on the site itself. The whole picture of your client's journey through your online world can be revealed to you, and that's worth more to your business than anything else. Spend a little time exploring so that you know what your clients want, when they want it, and what is important to them.

CHAPTER 9 FROM 30,000 FEET

Email marketing is cost effective, and you can do it without much time, budget, or technical know-how.

. . . .

Your business owns its email list, and you can take it to a different platform if one no longer works for you.

. . . .

Before composing your email marketing campaigns, ask what your most desired response (MDR) is, what business goal the email is supporting, and what value the message brings to the reader.

. . . .

Have people consented to being on your email marketing list? Do you have records of that consent?

. . . .

Have email marketing signup options available in a number of different places, including on your website and in your physical location.

. . . .

Experiment with A/B testing to determine what the best day and time to send an email campaign is, as well as which email subject lines result in more opens.

. . . .

Connect your email marketing program's reports to your website's analytics, so you can see the customer's entire journey from when they click an email, right through to the action they take on your website.

. . . .

10

Online Advertising

THINK ABOUT ALL the advertising you experienced today.

Start at the beginning. Your alarm clock goes off, and a catchy jingle from an ad on the local radio station gets stuck in your head before you can hit the snooze button. You roll over and grab your smartphone, scanning social media to see what happened in the world since you last checked. You see a few ads among the posts. On your morning commute, you're hit with more advertising—on billboard signs along the road, bus shelters, or in the middle of the podcast you're listening to.

At work, ad after ad is integrated into pretty much every website you visit. You go to the bathroom, and there's an ad in the stall. At lunch, you open up a magazine, flipping through dozens of pages of ads before you get to the articles.

You glance at the sticker on your banana—even your fruit has advertising on it.

Later, when you're relaxing at home, catching up on the latest TV drama, you try to fast-forward through the commercial breaks, but you can't help but see a few ads. You experience a dozen more ads before you finally go to sleep. And that's just the advertising you can recall.

ADVERTISING IS EXHAUSTING. We're bombarded with ads every day, and not all messages are remembered or even noticed. Any paid form of communication about a product, service, or business aim is considered to be advertising. Our world is filled with it!

That's why so many of us have become skeptical of the traditional advertising pitch. Many advertisers, in response, have begun to disguise their sales messages, abandoning that familiar pitch and embedding messages subtly into popular culture. Products appear regularly in television shows, on video and board games, and in movies. Ads are everywhere: according to a *New York Times* article, it's estimated that city dwellers see more than 5,000 ads every single day.

Think about how things have changed. Two generations ago, a driver might see a billboard while cruising down the highway. This billboard contained a single message, stretched tall and wide, and it captured their attention somewhat subliminally as they passed by. Regardless of what the brand advertising on the billboard was, a figment of its product or service was stored in the driver's mind. When movie-goers had a moment to stretch their legs, they were directly targeted by a singing and dancing snack—a not-so-subtle reminder that popcorn and soda were nearby. Advertising 40 to 60 years ago focused on getting the point across, both subliminally via graphics and jingles and intentionally with often long-winded arguments for a brand's worth. No longer is advertising so simple and charismatic. With greater variety in media have come greater issues in creating advertising that works.

The internet generation is a resourceful one, and they educate themselves about services and products that mean something to them (and they develop strong allegiances based on this research). The internet is a great place for product research. Social media is full of people asking for consumer advice. It's a natural environment for word-of-mouth advertising. That said, social media is also full of *influencers* who are paid by brands to endorse their products. While social media influencers are supposed to disclose their messages as ads, not all do.

Today's consumers are increasingly media smart about advertising and can sniff out ads better than ever before, whatever form they take. Even so, you can still be effective in an online ad environment without being sneaky, unethical, or annoying to your potential customers.

Successful advertising is all about reaching the right customer in the right moment. In a digital context, that's often when someone is seeking information about a product or service. In this chapter, we'll talk about how to achieve advertising goals in those online environments. We'll discuss ideas around generating advertising messages for the web, evaluating and selecting between them, and executing them effectively and responsibly.

Advertising decision-making

It's not an easy task to design a message that will gain attention. Time and thought must be given to the nature of the appeal, the actual words and images to be used, and the most appropriate platform for each campaign.

Online advertising has become more pointed, brief, and even attack-like in its predatory approach to forcing an audience to watch with pop-up videos, forced click ads, and website frames filled with affiliate links. By hoping to draw them in with something memorable, and if not, offer up a different morsel quickly before a consumer clicks away, companies have gone to extremes in recent years. So much online advertising feels like bombardment and drives people to turn on ad-blockers in order to avoid it all.

Let's talk about how to do this the right way. For online advertising, follow the same basic principles as in the previous chapter on email marketing. What's your core message, and what are you going to offer your clients? Remember these four important questions.

1   **Which business goal is this advertising campaign supporting?** How am I going to further my strategy by advertising to people who are interested in my products or services?

2   **What is the number-one message I want to convey in the advertising campaign, and what action do I want people to take?** What is my most desired response (MDR) for this campaign, and do I have any secondary goals beyond my MDR?

3 **What value does this advertising campaign bring to the viewer?** What's in it for someone to click on your ad? What do they get by seeing it and acting on it? Why would someone take action (ideally your MDR)? If you can't clearly state the value, then it won't be clear to the viewer.

4 **How will I measure the effectiveness of the advertising campaign?** It is likely that you'll only be tracking one or two metrics for your online advertising campaign: the key performance indicator that corresponds directly with your most desired response. If your MDR is "send people to our website and have them buy something," the metric you'll first look at is clickthrough rate. You will also want to track what happens after people click through to your site. Did they make a purchase? That's the second metric you'll look at: conversion rate. It's important to think about what metrics matter to you *most* and ignore the rest. That's because online advertising gives you so much information about performance, it can be confusing. If your MDR is sending people to your website to buy a product, then metrics such as the number of likes the ad received are not what you should be focusing on.

Answering these questions can clarify where you want to be when it comes to your next steps. That's because there are a few more essential decisions that you'll need to make: budget decisions and media decisions.

Platforms and costs

Different online advertising platforms offer different advantages and disadvantages, and cost is an important consideration. In general, the greater the number of eyeballs you can reach on a given platform, the higher the cost will be. Also, once you stop paying for ads, they disappear (duh). There's no lasting effect, so I don't recommend investing in online advertising as your only digital marketing effort. That having been said, online ads can be a quick way to drive a lot of traffic to your site (which in turn can boost your organic SEO) and may get you fast results while other forms of marketing take longer to come around.

Let's have a look at the online advertising platforms available to you.

Google Ads

Google's advertisements are some of the highest-quality paid traffic sources online. That's because of the fact that people are more likely to take action when they are actively searching for something, rather than when they're randomly exposed to a product or service. Search ads are Google's text advertisements that appear in the top of search engine results, and Display Network ads are image-based ads that appear on websites across the internet, where the owner of the website is selling a bit of real estate to Google (a.k.a. the Google Display Network). Google has the lion's share of search in Canada (90 percent) and in the United States (68 percent), as well as Gmail, YouTube, Google Maps, Google Shopping, Google Play, and partnerships with more than two million sites that show Google Ads (via the Display Network), which reach the majority of internet users every day.

Google Ads are, for the most part, ads that are connected to the content on your website, and the most common purpose of Google Ads is to drive traffic to a particular page of your site. You can even make "retargeting" or "remarketing" ads inside the Google Ads system: these are advertisements only shown to people who have visited your website before and can be used to remind them of what they saw or encourage them to come back to your site.

Running a successful Google Ads campaign is hard. They can be quite technical and need to be monitored closely. You may need professional support to make Google Ads effective for your business.

Other display networks

Beyond the Google Display Network, there are also niche and industry-specific display networks if you're trying to reach websites with a particular topic. For example, there are display networks for advertising on specific industry websites (like house and home lifestyle websites, or wedding industry websites) and it can be valuable to access this real estate if you happen to be in those lines of business.

One-off banner ads

If you want to advertise on a specific website, you may be able to get in touch with the site's owner and buy banner advertising space from them directly. This is a fairly common practice on news websites and blogs. Using banner ads is sometimes more challenging than you might expect. Although you can design your own graphics using low-cost tools like Canva (canva.com), you may need professional help with this, both to make effective creative advertising and to run the campaigns. It can be expensive, and it requires close monitoring: you need to pay attention to the communication and sales effects of advertising before, during, and after the ad runs. That having been said, it's common practice that when you buy banner ad space on a website, you either pay for the number of impressions (i.e., the number of people who saw the ad) or you pay for the number of clicks your ad receives. So, if it's a well-designed ad that attracts the right audience, it can be worth the effort.

Social media advertising: Boosting posts

As we talked about in the social media chapter, it can be hard for your social media posts to cut through algorithms that prioritize non-business content. One way to ensure your posts are being seen is to "boost" them. This means throwing a few dollars at Facebook to cut through the algorithm and ensures greater visibility for your posts. But does that mean you have to pay for every social media platform? Again, the answer lies in your vision and goals. Does your target client or customer hang out a lot on social media? In that case, you may want to pay to play. Trying a small amount of money (I suggest $5 at a time) before dropping bank can help you make the best decisions.

Facebook and Instagram ads

I've just mentioned boosting Facebook posts, but boosted posts are technically different from ads on Facebook (and Instagram, which Facebook owns). Boosting posts is what it sounds like—putting a bit of money behind the posts your business shares on Facebook, boosting the likelihood that they're seen by your Facebook followers.

Facebook ads are different. They're similar to Google Ads: they're a combo of graphics and text that can be shown in various places inside Facebook, Instagram, and Facebook's display network. You can create ads that appear in the Facebook News Feed, the Instagram Feed, on the sidebar of Facebook on laptop or desktop computers, and other spots inside the Facebook ecosystem. Facebook ads are powerful because you can target audiences based on a variety of criteria, including whether someone follows your organization's page or not, their gender, age, geographic location, interests, and more.

Once you've customized your advertising audience, you can send super-tailored advertising messages to each audience. Facebook advertising can be addictive—there's a reason why it's a multimillion-dollar revenue stream for the social networking giant. The options for building custom advertising audiences are robust, and the advertising performance reports that Facebook generates offer a lot of data. But remember just because something can be measured doesn't necessarily mean that measurement matters to you. Focus on the report that indicates whether you're achieving your business goal and ignore the other numbers.

CAUTION! GET YOUR HOUSE IN ORDER BEFORE BUILDING ONLINE ADS

AS WE'VE EXPLORED, online advertising can be great at driving traffic to your website. But before you start sending hordes of website visitors to your site, ask yourself if your site is optimized for that traffic. Is it mobile-friendly, fast, and accessible? (If not, go back to chapter 4.) Does your website have content that will speak to these website visitors, clearly laid out in a way that drives them to act? (If not, go back to chapter 6.)

My point here is you better be sure your house is in order and your website isn't a hot mess before you start putting money into online ads. Spending money on online ads that drive traffic to a subpar website is money wasted.

Now that you've thought long and hard

Online advertising can be amazing for high-growth phases of an organization (think launching a new product or service or launching in a new market). But what I hope you've learned in this chapter is that it's hard to keep an active advertising campaign going for small and medium businesses without deep pockets. Online advertising is a great tool in the digital marketing toolbox, but odds are you'll have to use it sparingly.

Start low and slow

Take your time getting to know the online advertising options you're excited about. Experiment with your ad spend and play around with the options available to you. Spend a little bit of money, monitor it closely, and try out some of the organic options listed here as well. At first, you're only looking for a signal in the noise. Throw spaghetti at the wall and see what sticks. Once you start to get a bit of positive impact with your MDRs, put more money on what works.

Advertising is speculation. That means it's exactly like going to the casino. You've got to find the game that works for you. Every game has a different set of rules, and a different amount of cash needed to buy in to the round. Some advertising platforms are like penny slots: you can spend a little and see modest results. Some online advertising options are like the high rollers' tables: they require a big buy-in, but the payoff can be huge. Only spend what you're comfortable losing!

In the end, what makes advertising work? You have to focus on the value you provide! Highlight what makes your business or product unique and competitive, and what you bring to the table that's different from everyone else. You're always going to win bigger if you can leverage discount prices, promotions, and exclusive offers, but you have to be really clear about your call to action. Phrases like "get a quote," "join now," or "call today" actually mean something. Just make sure that the words you choose mean something to your customer.

. . . .

CHAPTER 10 FROM 30,000 FEET

Advertising is everywhere, so make sure yours stands out.

. . . .

When planning online ads, ask yourself:

→ Which business goal is this advertising campaign supporting?
→ What is the number-one message I want to convey in the advertising campaign, and what action do I want people to take?

→ What value does this advertising campaign bring to
   the viewer?
→ How will I measure the effectiveness of the advertising campaign?

. . . .

Your online advertising platform options for a small
business include Google Ads, Facebook and Instagram
ads, other display networks, and one-off ads.

. . . .

Start by spending a little to see if you get any traction.
If you're seeing results, double down.

. . . .

11

Keeping Track and Measuring

WOW. WE'VE COVERED a lot. You now know how to build a mobile-friendly, fast, and accessible website; fill it with killer content; drive traffic from Google; build your brand on social media; and nurture your client and customer relationships through email marketing and online advertising. Speaking of client and customer relationships, how are you *managing* those? There's a digital solution, and you might want to consider it for your business.

Keeping track of customers and clients

I once worked with an organic farmer named Lucy who brought her delicious, farm-fresh vegetables to farmers' markets in and around Toronto. Lucy hired me to help build her email marketing strategy and paid me in tomatoes. No joke!

In order to get a better understanding of how Lucy interacted with her customers, I went to a few of the farmers' markets and watched how the transactions happened. One thing amazed me—Lucy knew so much about her customers. She knew who had a standing order and who got a discount because they're a loyal shopper. Lucy even knew the names of the dogs and children of some of her regulars.

I quickly realized that these relationships were as important to Lucy's business as the produce on the market table. People visited Lucy's stall at the farmers' market for the tomatoes (they really were phenomenal tomatoes) but also for the relationship they had with her.

I knew that Lucy wanted to scale her business and do even more farmers' markets, which meant she'd be bringing on a team member to help. It was essential that all of the things Lucy knew about her customers got out of her head and into a system.

———————————

A CRM IS a client or customer relationship management system. The emphasis of this kind of system is on the words "relationship" and "management." CRMs help you track of all your people and your relationships to them. The overall objective of a CRM is to stay organized as you find, attract, and gain new clients, and then retain and nurture those clients for long-term and beneficial relationships, while keeping efficiency and effectiveness in mind.

Think of a CRM as your brain but at scale.

It's not only a system to keep track of your clients and their purchase history but also to plan how to sell to your clients in the future. A CRM is like an electronic public relations diva who knows every single person you know and wants to invite everyone to the party.

What kind of CRM does your business need?

Let's take a step back and talk about what you need.

If you have an online store, it should be keeping track of all transactions, and giving you valuable data like which products are selling the most, what the average sales cycle is, what the average customer spends, how many people are new versus returning buyers, etc. That's wonderful. But you may need a separate solution to keep track of what *you* know about your customers or clients. That's where we start.

First and foremost, a CRM should be the place where all the information about your customers is stored. A CRM can be your customer service database, so members of your team can look up past clients and customers and see notes about their history. If this is how you want to use a CRM, it's essential that the system integrates with your communications channels, like your company email and social media. It also needs to coordinate with your online store or accounting solution, so you can see what the person has purchased or what they've been invoiced for. Finally, you'll need to be able to leave notes in the customer's or client's profile in the CRM, so you can share what you know about them with your team members internally.

Second, you can use your CRM as a marketing and communications hub. A CRM can centralize all the outbound communications to your customers or clients, such as your newsletters, sales announcements, events, and more. Many CRMs offer email marketing functionality, so you can send messages from within the system or integrate with another email marketing solution like Mailchimp.

One caveat, though.

Many CRMs are tailored for the sales industry, where relationship management is key. They include sales-specific features, like the ability to see your relationship with the client through a sales funnel. But even if you don't have a sales team, your business can benefit from a CRM. Just pick one that has functionality beyond sales management.

Which CRM should you use?

In the large (and still growing) market of CRM platforms, Salesforce has become a leader in the field; its Sales Cloud is a widely used application that helps organizations of all types manage and run their sales processes. Even though this software is fully customizable, it is inevitably going to have its pros and cons when a specific organization uses it for their operation. Other similarly sized CRM platforms include those offered by Oracle, HubSpot, and Microsoft. But these industry leaders, although they have very powerful features, are likely overkill for a small biz. Sure, Salesforce can work for a small business, but it's like shooting a mosquito with a cannon.

You might feel more comfortable with a CRM that is appropriate for your size and what you're doing with it. The big guys are likely too big (and too expensive!) for what you need. Smaller CRMs like Insightly, Nimble, and ZoHo work best for small businesses. Focus on the functionality you need right now, rather than paying too much for a monthly service with features you might never use.

Remember you will be able to take your client information with you if you ever have to change platforms or level up. Your data belongs to you, not your software provider.

You want a marriage, not a blind date

No matter what platform you use for your CRM, it's all about building relationships.

When you're building relationships with your clients, you need to think deeply about how to maintain those relationships over time. Nurturing your ties can make your relationship go from transactional to transcendent. Customer relationship management software can help you get there.

Metrics, metrics everywhere

If you've been following my advice so far, you could now be rocking your website, social media, email marketing, online advertising, and customer relationships. That's a *lot* of activity, and it's definitely taking some time, money, and resources to keep it going. How are you going to measure whether this effort is worthwhile?

You know what I'm going to say—you tie it back to your business goal. You pick a key performance indicator that lets you know if you're getting closer to that business goal. And you regularly check to see how you're doing. But where exactly do you look for that information?

Website metrics and Google Analytics

Metrics for your digital marketing efforts are usually found inside the tool you used to execute that digital marketing strategy. For example, the metrics for Facebook are inside Facebook. Same goes for Mailchimp.

What about your website, though? Some website builders (including Squarespace, Shopify, and WordPress.com) have reporting built in. But I don't recommend you rely on them, at least not solely. Use the gold standard of website measurement: Google Analytics. Generally speaking, Google Analytics has more reliable data than that found in website builders' reports. And when it comes to measurement and metrics, making sure you have clean, reliable data is essential. You're going to use this information to make business decisions! There's nothing worse than lacking confidence that your data is clean. Well, I guess a few things in this world are worse. But you get my point.

Google Analytics is a key tool for researching your current and ideal customer base, strategic plans, and long-term goals through detailed statistics about a website's traffic and traffic sources. It also measures conversions and sales. There is a paid version, but what you get for free is more than enough for most small businesses.

To get started, go to Analytics.Google.com and sign up for a free account. Here's the one technical thing: Google Analytics has to be "hooked up" to your website. You can do this by cutting and pasting the provided tracking code into your site; Google will tell you the correct place to put this, or you can get a developer's assistance to do it. You can also check to see if there's an integration for your type of website, which may be your easiest option if you aren't comfortable dropping some code into your site. For example, you can use a plugin for Google Analytics to connect to a WordPress site or a Shopify app to connect it to a Shopify site. In any case, it takes a second to get this done.

Once you have it hooked up and you're ready to explore Google Analytics, you'll find the main areas in the reporting section are Audience, Acquisition, Behaviour, and Conversions.

The **Audience** section provides you with a wonderful snapshot of who's visiting your website: where they live, what languages they speak, whether they've visited your site only once or many times, and how many of them are out there, hanging on your every word.

The **Acquisition** section looks at how people got to your site in the first place. It helps you understand whether people are finding you through search, through a social media site, or through a third-party site like an editorial or article about your organization. Clicks to your site are critical because they show how and when a person's awareness about your organization or brand can convert them to potential client.

Behaviour data tracks what people are doing while visiting your site. It looks at where they go within the site, what pages are the most popular, and where people linger over information. This shows you what matters to your visitors so that you can take advantage of where they want to hang out; it can help you answer questions as to what is important to them so that you can provide more of it. Behaviour reports show you pageview rates and time-on-page over time, drawing out the top content. It also includes what is known as a bounce rate, which is something that many people seem to be overly concerned about. (That's why I've written a little sidebar about that particular statistic.)

Conversion data is about tracking exactly when an individual either becomes or becomes one step closer to being a customer or client. You have to set up a "goal" for Google Analytics to track as a conversion—making an online sale, filling out a contact form and clicking the submit button, or some other measurable indication of interest.

BOUNCE! BOUNCE!

LET'S TALK ABOUT bounce rate and clear the air. It's the one metric inside Google Analytics that all the small businesses I work with are always asking about. The bounce rate is the percentage of visitors who come to your website and then leave after viewing only one webpage (the one they saw when they came to the site in the first place). There's a feeling that a high bounce rate (70 percent or higher) is bad. That's because of a long-standing rumour that a high bounce rate is bad for your website's SEO.

This is debateable. (Literally—professional SEO experts debate this topic regularly.) A high bounce rate, on its own, will not affect your search engine results in a strong way. Consider a webpage that has all the information someone might be looking for, without having to click off the page. Perhaps it's a one-page website and that's all there is, or perhaps the website visitor found everything they needed and then they moved on. For example, a Wikipedia entry would have a high bounce rate, but it's not a "bad" webpage! If the goal of a webpage is to share information, then a high(ish) bounce rate isn't a bad thing.

A high bounce rate *can*, however, be an indicator of other issues with a website that could be more nefarious (and have a negative impact on your site's SEO). A high bounce rate could indicate that visitors left the site because it was slow to load, or it didn't render well on a mobile device, or it had poorly written or unsatisfying content. There may be a dissonance between what your site is saying and the traffic it's attracting. If your site has a bounce rate of more than 50 percent, then I encourage you to think about why. If your goals are information based or educational, then it's likely fine. But if your bounce rate is above 50 percent and your goal is to have people click through the site and eventually take an action (like make a purchase or click a contact link), then you may need to do a deeper investigation into what's going on.

Social media metrics

We touched on this a bit in the social media chapter, but let's get into even more detail here. Social media metrics can show you when someone is on their journey from discovery of your business to potentially becoming a client or customer. At a high level, this is what that journey looks like for most:

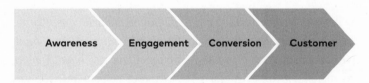

We can take those four sections (Awareness, Engagement, Conversion, and Customer) and line them up with metrics you can find inside social media measurement.

- Awareness metrics: mentions, audience growth over time, reach

- Engagement metrics: approval or applause actions (likes, favourites), engagement actions (comments), amplification actions (shares, retweets)

- Conversion metrics: clicks, phone calls, emails, sales

- Customer metrics: reviews and testimonials

Not sure what all these terms mean? No problem. Let's define them.

Awareness metrics include mentions, reach, and impressions.

- **Mentions** are when someone mentions your business name on social media (either by tagging your social media handle or just typing your name). It's an obvious indicator of brand awareness.

- **Reach** is the number of people that *could* see your social media posts.

- This contrasts with what are called **impressions**, which are the number of times your message is displayed and *potentially* seen, whether or not someone actually really sees it.

This is an important point about these metrics, so listen up. When you are on Facebook or Twitter, do you read every post or tweet? Nope. You scan through them. Reach means that the particular post or tweet is *available* to you. Like, it exists because you have subscribed to that person's feed. Whether or not you are online that day is irrelevant to reach. Impressions means that the particular post or tweet is in your feed. You may or may not notice it when scanning through your feed, but it's *there*.

Reach and impressions can definitely indicate brand awareness, but they can also be dangerous. See the sidebar about vanity metrics and keep that in mind. If you're deep in the awareness stage of brand building for your business, it's okay to focus on reach and impressions. But don't get stuck there.

CAUTION! VANITY METRICS

UNLESS YOUR ONLY goal is brand building and creating awareness for your organization on social media, a lot of the metrics in social media (like follower count, reach, and impressions) are simply an exercise in vanity. Vanity metrics are the numbers that make us feel good. They're the measurements that can make you feel high-school popular, important, or impressive, but they don't indicate whether you're closer to your goal or not. Obsessing over vanity metrics is an easy trap to fall into. Sure, you can look at them and feel a little ego rush, but don't confuse them with the measurements that will really tell you how your business is doing.

Don't look in that vanity mirror unless you just want to see how pretty you are! In most cases, instead of focusing on vanity's siren call to look at your follower count, reach, or impressions on social media, focus on engagement and conversion and what is happening in your actual bank account, store location, or client list as the result of your social media efforts. Remember back in the social media chapter when I talked about the trap of social, and how it can be like treading water? If you have low engagement or low conversion, this is a key indicator that you're treading water and not getting closer to the shore.

Engagement metrics are what we often see before some-one converts to becoming a customer or client, and they can be broken down into three areas: approval or applause actions, engagement actions, and amplification actions. These are listed in order of power and importance.

- **Approval or applause actions** include people clicking the "like" or "favourite" button in reaction to your social media post. This requires the least amount of commit-ment from someone and is a good, but fairly casual, indicator of their interest.

- On the other hand, leaving a comment (an **engagement action**) is a greater indicator of engagement with a business. It shows that someone has taken the time to respond to what you're saying, and that's a big deal.

- The biggest indicator of engagement in social media, though, is an **amplification action**. This means someone has an opinion about what you have to say that's strong enough for them to pass it on to their own social media followers. This could be done by clicking the "share" button, retweeting, or reposting your message, or for-warding it on to someone through a direct message (DM).

Conversion metrics are the ones that you're likely track-ing already, whether you're even aware of it. Of course, the number-one conversion metric that matters most to small businesses is sales. This is often indicated through a click online—a click to purchase, a click to call or email, or a click to submit a form response.

Customer metrics are important too. When someone be-comes a customer or client, that's not the end of the journey—in many ways, it's just beginning! Customer metrics are measurements that indicate the health of your relationship with existing customers. You want to maintain those relationships so that people buy from you again and refer you to their friends. This can be tracked on social media through reviews and testimonials, which some social platforms offer.

Pick a small handful of social media metrics to focus on, based on where the majority of your customers are and where you are in your business growth. Remember these should tie back to your business goal. If you're trying to launch in a new market, then you're going to focus on awareness metrics. Already established and want to get people talking about you? Engagement metrics will tell you if you're moving in the right direction.

Connecting the data points

Remember that the whole point of metrics and measurements is to see how you're doing. It's so easy to get distracted by the piles of data at your fingertips, but remember that most of it is noise! You're looking for a signal in that noise. It takes discipline to put on blinders and focus, but it gets easier with time. How often should you check your metrics? I recommend at least every week. You can set Google Analytics to send you any report you like by email at a regular interval. Get those reports every week and actually look at them. Chart them over time and look for the larger trends.

And don't forget about offline metrics. There's a tendency to think that everything has to be digital, but unless your business is 100 percent online, you have offline metrics too. Don't discount them—sometimes they are the right metric to measure your success. Consider metrics like foot traffic in your store or how many times the phone rings in your office, as a means to determine if what you're doing is making an impact.

Let's review. For every initiative you want to keep an eye on, follow these five steps.

1   **Identify key indicators.** Are you looking to drive revenue or build awareness of your brand? Your answer determines what success will look like in your data, so write this down.

2   **Align your goals with very specific objectives.** For any campaign to be meaningful and measurable, you've got to break down the big picture into smaller, bite-sized goals.

3   **Track actions.** Set up systems for tracking and monitor how often clients or customers complete the actions you define—and set aside the vanity mirror.

4   **Assign values to your indicators.** Once you have chosen your goals and set up your tracking, it's time to tackle the values of these goals, and how much time and money it'll take you to achieve them. Decide what matters to you over the short and the long term, and match your goals to where you are in your business growth cycle.

5   **Benchmark and learn.** You can compare yourself to yourself (this is why we measure where we're starting from), or you can compare your efforts to your competitors to uncover opportunities for your organization to stand out and be heard through the noise. Over time, you can learn what platforms are most successful in reaching your target audience and what makes an impact on your bottom line and organizational sustainability.

As a small but mighty business owner, you can (and will!) achieve your goals, but those goals are going to change over time as you develop your ideas and test your strategies and web opportunities.

Let them change! You don't need to be tied down to a single metric for measurement, just as you don't need to be tied down to selling one product or running the same event every single year. Your business will evolve along with your skills, your audience, and your ideas. Experiment in order to understand what works and keep on keeping on.

. . . .

CHAPTER 11 FROM 30,000 FEET

If you're keeping track of customer or client information in your head, you need a CRM system.

. . . .

Look at functionality and price when considering CRM solutions, and don't be afraid to go with a smaller choice like Insightly, Nimble, or ZoHo if that's all you need.

. . . .

Connect your website to Google Analytics for insight into your website traffic.

. . . .

To gain insight into your social media reports, pick the metrics that relate to the four stages of the customer journey: Awareness, Engagement, Conversion, and Customer.

. . . .

Beware of vanity metrics!

. . . .

12

Bringing It All Together

ALRIGHT, ALRIGHT. WE'RE almost done. But before we finish up, I have one more story to tell, and then we're going to talk about how to make your overarching digital plan come to life.

We're all the same

When I first sat down to write this book, I thought I'd have different sections for all different sizes and types of small businesses, because there are so many! In fact, Gartner, the global research and advisory firm, tells us that "small businesses are usually defined as organizations with fewer than 100 employees" and "small business is usually defined as organizations with less than $50 million in annual revenue."

From 1 to 100 employees and from $1 to $50 million in revenue are *huge* ranges! I envisioned myself doling out specific tech advice for the micro businesses, the businesses with a handful of employees, the businesses with fast growth, and the businesses that had been around for a while with a heap of employees.

The funny thing was, while I was writing, I found I was giving the same core advice to each type of organization.

- Follow the framework of Goal > Plan > Execute > Measure > Learn.
- Don't build your castle on someone else's land.
- Focus on a small number of key metrics to see how you're doing.
- Look for the signal in the noise to determine what's working, and then double down on those efforts.
- Stay open to learning new things.
- Get comfortable with being uncomfortable.

So, here we are at the end of the book that ended up emerging instead. I've been running my own small business in some form or other for more than 14 years now, and what you've read here is the advice I knew I had to give to *all* of you, whether you're working on a side business, a micro biz, or building your empire with dozens of employees and millions in revenue.

The cool part about everything in this book is that the advice scales. One thing I can tell you for sure is that the only constant in life is change. It used to terrify me, but now I welcome it—it's exciting! Business will change. Your goals will change. Technology will *most definitely* change. The small business owners I see thriving are the ones who embrace change, or at least build a resiliency to it. But the advice remains the same; just adjust it to your new situation.

Wash, rinse, repeat.

Your digital transformation

So, at the end of it all, I want you to gather your thoughts and write down exactly what it is that you're going to do. Right now.

Carving out time for yourself and for the big questions that you have chosen to ask and pursue is a critical first step to your digital transformation. Let's map it all out before you begin, so you can see the whole picture. Put on your favourite music, pour a cup of tea, and let's dive in.

Question 1: What are your goals?

What are your business or organizational goals? Where do you want to go with your company in a year or in five years? What do you want to achieve for yourself and for your clients and customers? For most small business owners, the answer is usually "I want to make more money." Go further than that with more detail. Examples of common small business goals include:

- Expand into a new geographic area by opening an additional physical location

- Reach customers or clients outside your geographic area by selling online

- Offer a follow-up service to existing or past clients who want to continue to engage with your company

- Attract a new client base for a premium product or service, so you can increase profit margins

Question 2: How do your goals inform your strategy?

How can you translate your business goals into a digital strategy? With everything you now know about digital marketing, what do you want to focus on? What digital levers do you think you can pull to get you closer to your business goal? Consider doing the following things:

- Enhance your website's SEO to drive more traffic to your online store from organic search (and therefore sell more products)

- Grow your email list to reach current and past clients, keeping them updated on what you're doing (so they will continue to enlist your services)

- Run a set of Facebook and Instagram ads targeting a specific demographic, with polished images and captivating copywriting, to make your premium product covetable (so you can sell more of it)

Question 3: What's your KPI?

Now that you have a sense of what area of digital marketing you're going to focus on, decide which key performance indicator (KPI) you're going to track. What is the one metric that will determine whether you're getting closer to your business goal or not? What are the one or two supporting metrics that also indicate if you're on the right path? Consider:

- Number of sales
- Number of people who physically visit your store every day
- Number of phone calls you receive
- Number of visits to particular pages of your website

- Number of email signups
- Email open rate
- Clickthrough rate of online ads

Question 4: Where are you right now?

The only way to know how far you've gone is to establish where you started. Take the KPI you identified in Question 3, and ask, "Where are we right now?" First, figure out where you're going to find your KPI. Is it inside Google Analytics? Inside your email marketing program? Inside social media? Inside your CRM software? Once you find it, write down the current value. You're going to need this for reflection later.

Question 5: What are you going to do, and how much are you going to spend?

Don't dive in and get going—at least not yet. First, you have to make a plan. What exactly are you going to do? How much time and money will it cost? How long will it take to test, and how much time will you invest before deciding whether or not it's working?

Make a budget (for both time spent and actual dollars) for your web presence, your digital advertising, your software and newsletters, and your social media. Be realistic and detailed, and don't bite off more than you can chew. Start with what's achievable. You can always add more later.

Question 6: How and when will you check the KPI?

What's your plan for measurement? How often will you need to check your KPI, and how will you remember to do so? Set a reminder or a recurring event in your calendar to regularly check your KPI.

It's go time

After you've made your way through this book and these six questions, you've planned as much as you possibly can. It's time to leap. Your plan won't be perfect, and there will be unknowns. But you're as well equipped as you can be, and it's time to get started. Jump in the driver's seat, buckle up, and hit the gas. How fast you go is up to you. You can move through the stages of Goal > Plan > Execute > Measure > Learn as quickly or as slowly as you'd like. You're in control here. I believe in you.

Acknowledgements

NOTHING GREAT IS done alone, and that certainly includes the creation of this book. I owe a large amount of thanks to so many for helping *See You on the Internet* along its way.

From the moment I suspected I had a book in me, two women have supported me with all of the resources they could offer. The first is my business coach, Danielle Botterell. She has been my champion, my adversary, and my sage advisor. I hope all you business owners can find yourself a business coach like her. I am grateful to have you in my corner, Danielle.

The second Wonder Woman is Sara Angel. When I had a first draft of a book proposal, I sat on Sara's porch, soaking up her invaluable advice. From introducing me to agents and editors to reading early chapter drafts, Sara has been a cheerleader and confidante. I'm lucky to have you as a friend, Sara. Thank you.

There is a large group of professionals at the top of their game that I have been fortunate to work with. These people are the dream team. Samantha Haywood, Rob Firing, and

Stephanie Sinclair at Transatlantic Agency: I had heard you were the best, and now I know it. Thank you for all your work so far, and for the work to come.

Page Two is helmed by two smart, badass women who are changing the publishing industry, and it's easy to see why. It has been a delight to work with Trena White, Annemarie Tempelman-Kluit, Gabrielle Narsted, Peter Cocking, Taysia Louie, Deanna Roney, and Crissy Calhoun on this book. You are all consummate professionals, and it has been a true pleasure. Thank you for your expertise and patience with this first-time writer. Let's do it again soon, yeah?

Special thanks to Lisa Thomas-Tench for your help in the early stages of the proposal and manuscript development.

I want to extend a major thank-you to James Harbeck, substantive editor extraordinaire, for mixing the perfect amount of support, praise, and suggestions to take my manuscript from "meh" to "hell yeah!" I owe you a night out at the theatre.

Thank you to Sarah Efron, my editor at *The Globe and Mail*. Sarah took a chance on me, someone who had never written anything professionally in her life, and published it in the national newspaper of record. Your commitment to small businesses and exceptional journalism is admirable. I love working with you.

To Zoe Grams: there's no one else I would want to help promote this book. I deeply respect your work and your commitment to your values. You are proof that small businesses can make a difference in so many ways.

To Spencer Saunders and Stacey May Fowles: I'm glad I bumped into you at the Toronto Flower Market that day, because your suggestion is what led me to Zoe. You're good friends to have!

Speaking of good friends, I want to shout out to Shannon Lee Simmons and Amanda Munday, my writer friends who paved the path for me. When I submitted the first fully completed manuscript to James for editing, I immediately emailed Shannon and Amanda to say, "I DID IT!!!" and they both emailed back, "That's right you did!" No one understands the way they understand. Hugs and high fives to you both.

For the longest time, this book was known as *Avery Swartz's Untitled Digital Marketing and Tech Book* because I couldn't, for the life of me, settle on a proper title. Brainstorming with Helen Tremethick and Lianne George is what led me to *See You on the Internet*. Thank you both for generously donating your creativity and insight. Call me when your computers break and I'll fix them for free.

Thank you to Jess Joyce and Linn Øyen Farley for being early readers and being valuable fact checkers and gut checkers for some of the technical points in this book.

Special thanks to Crystal Chionidis, senior associate at GCSE LLP, for helping me finally learn proper bookkeeping and accounting principles. The story at the beginning of this book is 100 percent true. It was hell on wheels, but I got there eventually, and I couldn't have done it without you.

Not every moment in the writing of this book was a cakewalk. There were a few times where it got really tough, and in those moments, there are three people who helped me in ways I don't think I can ever truly repay.

Sarah Brohman, my wonderful friend who just happens to be a highly accomplished and experienced substantive editor, rescued me in an anxiety-fuelled moment when I had little confidence. I knew my manuscript needed help, but I couldn't see the next step. I literally googled, "I hate my book, what do I do?" I discovered a subreddit of authors who loathe their creations, which was interesting, but not particularly helpful. I emailed Sarah, who wrote the most wonderful response, clearly explaining to me that what I was feeling was normal and helping me to see what the next steps were. I'm so glad to have your guidance and friendship, Sarah.

On the same night I wrote that email to Sarah, I reached out to Melissa and Johnathan Nightingale, dear friends who had published their own book. They said, "We're putting our little kid to bed. Grab a bottle of Caol Ila and come over and sit in our living room and tell us what's going on." Between their compassion, gentle coaching, and a few drams of whisky, I went from "I don't know if I can do this" to "I think I might be able to do this." I love you and thank you.

To Sarah Stockdale and Christina Hug, who along with Melissa and Johnathan, form "the Fauxworkers": you are the ones I share the top 10 and bottom 10 percent of my personal and professional life with, and I love how we hold space for each other. I am so grateful for the Fauxs.

To Tara Wilkins, who makes everything work at Camp Tech. Years ago, you showed up one day, offering to volunteer and help out any way you could. Your commitment to your work, to the company, and to me is unparalleled. I don't know where I'll be working in the future, but I hope it's with you, Tara. May you always be the 4 to my 8.

To Dad and Jan, for unconditionally supporting me always, and also for putting that gazebo in your backyard. It's a writer's paradise and I did some of my best editing in that gazebo. I love you.

To my strong and brave daughter, Clara. Your ability to do new things even though you're scared is so inspiring. You amaze me. I love you so much.

And, finally, to Ian, my husband, my chef, my partner, my love. Nothing works without you. You make me live. You're my best friend.

Index

A/B testing, 155, 158
accessibility, website, 63–66, 68
accounting, 1–2, 53
Ad Standards' Influencer Market-
    ing Disclosure Guidelines, 115
advertising. *See* online advertising
alt text, 65–66
AMA (ask me anything) sessions,
    128–29
Amazon, 50
amplification action, 182
animation, 66
anti-virus software, 75
approval or applause actions, 182
awareness metrics, 180–81

backlinking, 111
banner ads, 165–66
behind-the-scenes look, 127, 129
BigCommerce, 45, 51
bloggers and social media influ-
    encers, 113–15, 161
blogs, 97, 98–99
boosting posts, 166
bounce rate, 177, 178–79
budgets. *See* finances and costs
Buffer, 96, 133

business goals: alignment with
    marketing strategy, 5, 17, 190;
    development, 8, 189; email
    marketing and, 153, 156; and
    metrics and measurement, 175,
    184; online advertising and,
    162; social media and, 125, 135,
    183; website and, 36, 67

Camp Tech: accounting experi-
    ence, 1–2, 53; background,
    3–4; search engine optimiza-
    tion (SEO) experience, 113–14,
    115, 116; website experience,
    61–62
Canada, data and anti-spam laws,
    79, 81, 143–44, 152
Canada's Anti-Spam Legislation
    (CASL), 79, 143–44, 152
change, 188–89
clickthrough rate, 153–54, 156–57
clients. *See* customers
cloud computing, 76
consent, 80, 81, 143–44, 158
content, 87–101; introduction and
    key points, 87–88, 100–101;
    being yourself, 93; blogs,

98–99; copywriting, 94–98; for email marketing, 148–49; guest appearances, 100; images, 93–94, 97; keywords, 91–92, 108–9; live streaming, 99–100; podcasting, 100; for social media, 125–30; style and voice, 89–91; updating content, 97; video, 99. *See also* search engine optimization (SEO)

content management systems (CMS), 45

contests and giveaways, 126–27

conversion, 154, 157, 177

conversion metrics, 136, 182

copywriting, 94–98

CoSchedule, 95–96

costs. *See* finances and costs

Creative Commons, 94

customer data, 77–84; introduction and key points, 77–78, 85; legislation on, 79–80; privacy policy, 82–84; purpose for collection, 81; responsibility for, 78–79; storage locations and exposure, 80–81; third-party data processors and, 82; tracking website visitors, 81–82

customer relationship management (CRM), 171–75; introduction and key points, 171–72, 185; effective use of, 175; purpose, 172–73; software options, 174; types of, 173–74

customers: customer metrics, 182–83; spotlight on social media, 129

data: data breaches, 72; data processors and data processing agreements (DPAs), 82; sharing on social media, 127. *See also* customer data; metrics and measurement

digital marketing: introduction and conclusion, 1–6, 187–92; Camp Tech for, 3–4; content, 87–101; creating a plan for, 189–91; customer relationship management (CRM), 171–75; digital security, 69–85; domain names, 20–27, 31; email hosting, 28–30; email marketing, 139–58; framework for, 7–17; metrics and measurements, 175–85; online advertising, 159–70; scalability of, 188–89; search engine optimization (SEO), 103–16; social media, 117–37; universal applicability, 187–88; website hosting, 27–28; websites, 33–68. *See also specific topics*

digital marketing framework, 7–17; introduction and key points, 7–8, 17; business goals, 8, 17; health food store example, 12, 13–14; as iterative cycle, 13–14; key performance indicators (KPIs), 9, 14; leaps, 10–11; learning, 11; measurement before and after marketing efforts, 10, 11; overview of steps, 8–11; skipping the process, 15–17

digital security, 69–85; introduction and key points, 69–71, 84–85; anti-virus software, 75; creating a plan for, 77; customer data, 77–84; data breaches, 72; malware and ransomware, 72; password management, 72–74; phishing,

71–72; practicing digital
hygiene, 76–77; privacy policy,
82–84; protecting yourself,
72–77; responsibility for, 71;
software updates, 74–75; third-
party data processors, 82;
two-factor authentication, 77;
using tools for, 75–76; virtual
private network (VPN), 75. *See
also* customer data
domain name registrars, 23
domain names, 20–27; introduction and key points, 20–21, 31;
author's collection of, 21; how
it works, 22; owning multiple
domains, 24; record keeping,
26–27; registration process
and considerations, 23–26

ecommerce, 49–55; introduction,
49; add-on to existing website,
49–50; external marketplaces,
50–51; integrations, 53–55;
payment gateway, 52; Shopify
for, 49, 51; store location,
49–51; website as store, 51
editorial content calendars, 133
elevator pitch, 89
email: digital hygiene with, 76;
email addresses, 30; email
hosting, 28–30, 31
email marketing, 139–58; introduction and key points, 139–41,
158; alignment with business
goals, 153, 156; clickthrough
rate, 153–54, 156–57; content,
148–49; conversion, 154, 157;
development process, 152–54;
email services for, 151–52,
155–56; experimentation and
testing, 154–56; integrations,
54, 157; legal considerations,

143–44; list segmentation,
147–48; Mailchimp, 152, 157;
meeting recipients' needs and
interests, 142–43, 149–51, 153;
metrics and measurement,
153–54, 156–57; mobile-first
design, 152, 155; most desired
response (MDR), 141–42, 153;
open rate, 153, 156; permission-
based email marketing,
144–45; role within digital
marketing strategy, 141–45;
soliciting subscribers, 145–47;
value of, 140–41
engagement action, 182
engagement metrics, 182
Etsy, 50
European Union's General Data
Protection Regulation (GDPR),
79–80, 81, 84, 144, 152
Eventbrite, 61–62

Facebook, 34–35, 119–20,
166–67, 175
finances and costs: budget for
digital marketing, 191; for
online advertising, 164–67; for
payment gateways, 52; for websites, 43–44
500px, 94
Flash, 57–58
#FlashbackFriday, 128

Gartner, 187
General Data Protection Regulation (GDPR), 79–80, 81, 84,
144, 152
gift guides and wish lists, 127
giveaways and contests, 126–27
goals. *See* business goals
GoDaddy (domain name
registrar), 23

GoDaddy Website Builder, 45
Google: Google Ads, 112–13,
    164–65; Google Analytics,
    157, 175–77, 183, 185; Google
    My Business, 112; G Suite,
    29; search algorithms, 103–4,
    105–7; tools for website perfor-
    mance diagnostics, 63
guest appearances, 100

Hootsuite, 133
hosting: email, 28–30, 31; website,
    27–28, 31
Hover.com, 23
how-to (instructional) posts, 128
HubSpot, 174

images, 93–94, 97
impressions, 180–81
inbound links, 110–11
Influencer Marketing Disclosure
    Guidelines (Ad Standards), 115
influencers, social media, 113–15, 161
information technology (IT), 70–71
Insightly, 174
Instagram, 123–24, 128, 129–30,
    166–67
instructional (how-to) posts, 128
integrations, 53–55, 56, 157
Internet Corporation for Assigned
    Names and Numbers
    (ICANN), 23
internet friends, 113, 130
Internet Protocol (IP) address, 22
internet service providers (ISPs), 78
Iubenda, 82

key performance indicators (KPIs),
    9, 11, 14, 36–37, 137, 184,
    190–91
keywords, 91–92, 108–10

landing pages, 44

LastPass, 73
leaps, 10–11
LinkedIn, 74, 119, 123, 127
live streaming, 99–100, 128–29

Magento, 51
Mailchimp, 152, 157, 175
malware, 72
mentions, 180
metadata, 59, 105
metrics and measurement, 175–85;
    introduction and key points,
    4–5, 175, 185; awareness
    metrics, 180–81; before and
    after marketing efforts, 10,
    11; bounce rate, 177, 178–79;
    business goals and, 175, 184;
    conversion metrics, 182; cre-
    ating a plan for, 191; customer
    metrics, 182–83; for email
    marketing, 153–54, 156–57,
    158; engagement metrics, 182;
    Google Analytics, 157, 175–77,
    183; key performance indica-
    tors (KPIs), 9, 11, 14, 36–37,
    137, 184, 190–91; offline met-
    rics, 183; for online advertising,
    163, 167; process and consid-
    erations, 183–85; for social
    media, 135–36, 179–83, 185;
    vanity metrics, 181; for web-
    sites, 36–37, 175–77, 183
Microsoft, 29–30, 174
milestones, sharing of, 130
Moneris, 52
most desired response (MDR),
    141–42, 153, 162
Myspace, 35

Nielsen, 96
Nimble, 174

Office 365 (Microsoft), 29–30

offline metrics, 183
1Password, 73
online advertising, 159–70; intro-
    duction and key points, 159–61,
    169–70; appropriate use, 168–
    69; banner ads, 165–66;
    boosting posts, 166; decision-
    making process, 162–63;
    Facebook and Instagram ads,
    166–67; Google Ads, 112–13,
    164–65; metrics and measure-
    ment, 163, 167; niche display
    networks, 165; platforms and
    costs, 164–67; search engine
    optimization (SEO) and, 112–
    13, 164; website optimization
    for, 167–68
online software creators, 79
open rate, 153, 156
Oracle, 174

PageRank, 110–11
password management, 72–74
payment gateways, 52, 56
PayPal, 50, 52
Personal Information Protection
    and Electronic Documents Act
    (PIPEDA), 79, 81
phishing, 71–72
Pinterest, 124–25
podcasting, 100
polls and quizzes, 129–30
privacy policy, 82–84

Q&A sessions, 128–29
QuickBooks, 53
quizzes and polls, 129–30

ransomware, 72
reach, 180–81
responsive design, 60–61, 67
reviews, from customers, 129

Salesforce, 174
search engine marketing (SEM), 107
search engine optimization (SEO),
    103–16; introduction and key
    points, 103–5, 116; backlink-
    ing, 111; black-hat solutions,
    107; bloggers and social media
    influencers, 113–15; Camp
    Tech's experience, 113–14, 115;
    components of, 108–13; defi-
    nition, 105; Google Ads and,
    112–13; Google's search algo-
    rithms, 103–4, 105–7; internet
    friends, 113; keywords and,
    92, 108–10; local SEO, 111–12;
    off-page SEO, 110–11; online
    advertising and, 112–13, 164;
    on-page SEO, 108–9; PageRank
    and inbound links, 110–11;
    Pinterest and, 124
security. See customer data;
    digital security
shipping integrations, 54–55
Shopify: Camp Tech experience,
    62; for ecommerce, 51, 55;
    integrations, 53; payment
    gateway, 52; website hosting,
    28; website metrics, 175–76;
    as website platform, 45, 49, 61
Shutterstock, 94
Signal, 76
small businesses, 187–88
social media, 117–37; introduction
    and key points, 117–19, 136–37;
    automation, 131–32; caution
    with, 134–35; choosing plat-
    forms, 118–19, 125; content,
    125–30; culture and etiquette,
    130–32; editorial content cal-
    endars, 133; Facebook, 119–20;
    guidelines and policy doc-
    ument, 132; influencers on,

113–15, 161; Instagram, 123–24; integrations, 54; LinkedIn, 123; management tools, 133–34; metrics and measurement, 135–36, 179–83, 185; overview of platforms, 119–25; Pinterest, 124–25; scheduling posts, 133–34; Twitter, 121–22; YouTube, 121; zombie accounts, 125
software updates, 74–75
speed, website, 63, 67
Sprout Social, 133
Squarespace, 28, 44–45, 48, 50, 55, 61, 175–76
statistics, sharing on social media, 127
Stripe, 50, 52
Sucuri, 70

team, spotlight on, 129
testimonials, 129
#ThrowbackThursday, 128
Twitter, 121–22, 128, 129–30
two-factor authentication, 77

United States of America, data and anti-spam laws, 79
Unsplash, 94
user-generated content, 127–28

vanity metrics, 181
video, 66, 99
virtual private network (VPN), 75

WAVE Web Accessibility Evaluation Tool, 64
Web Content Accessibility Guidelines (WCAG) 2.0, 64
website conventions, 39, 40, 65
website designers, 37
website developers, 37
websites, 19–31, 33–68; introduction and key points, 19–20, 31, 33–34, 55–56, 57–58, 67–68; accessibility, 63–66; bounce rate, 177, 178–79; costs, 43–44; creating your own, 44–49; designers vs. developers, 37; domain names, 20–27; ecommerce, 49–55; elements of good design, 38–39; hiring someone to create, 37–38, 39–44; hosting, 27–28, 31; integrations, 53–55; landing pages, 44; metadata, 59, 105; metrics and measurement, 35–37, 175–77, 183; optimization for mobile and other devices, 58–59, 59–61; optimization for online advertising, 167–68; payment gateways, 52; privacy policy, 82–84; reasons for, 34–35; responsive design, 60–61; Shopify, 49, 51; speed, 63; Squarespace, 48; tracking visitors, 81–82; trusting yourself, 66–67; updating websites, 61–62; WordPress, 45–48. *See also* content; digital security
Weebly, 45
Wirecutter, 75
wish lists and gift guides, 127
Wix, 45
WordPress, 44–45, 45–48, 50, 55, 175–76

Xero, 53

YouTube, 98–99, 121

ZoHo, 174
Zuckerberg, Mark, 74

About the Author

AVERY SWARTZ IS the founder and CEO of Camp Tech, which offers digital marketing training for small businesses, non-profits, and those curious to learn more about technology. She was ranked number five on *Search Engine Journal*'s Top 50 Women in Marketing list. Avery is the resident tech expert on CTV's *Your Morning*, highlighting the latest tech gadgets, apps, and tech news for a national audience. She writes for *Chatelaine*, *Today's Parent*, and *The Globe and Mail* on tech topics for modern women, families, and small businesses. Avery has been a professor at both Ryerson University and Humber College. She lives in Toronto.

. . . .

seeyouontheinternet.com
averyswartz.com
camptech.ca